THE PARENTS' BOOK OF CHECKLISTS

FROM TODDLERS TO TEENAGERS

SALLY COULTHARD

PEARSON

Prentice Hall

LIFE

Pearson Education Limited
Edinburgh Gate
Harlow
Essex CM20 2JE
England

ISBN 978-0-273-71279-4

Commissioning editor: Emma Shackleton
Project editor: Patricia Burgess
Copy editor: Jeanette Payne
Designer: Kevin O'Connor
Cover design: R&D&Co
Senior production controller: Man Fai Lau

Printed and bound by Henry Ling, UK

The Publisher's policy is to use paper manufactured from sustainable
forests.

Contents

Contents

Introduction

When you're a new parent you long for the day when your child reaches toddlerhood. Perhaps then, you imagine, your child will be able to communicate what's wrong and make the process of parenting that little bit easier.

The reality is that each new stage of parenting, whether it's preschool or puberty, brings its own set of challenges and joys. I don't think there's ever a point at which parenting becomes a doddle – but that's part of the fun.

This book is designed to take some of the mystery out of the many different situations that characterize childhood and adolescence. Some are obvious, such as starting school and bedwetting. But I've also tried to include some checklists about the more subtle aspects of parenting a growing child, such as developing his emotional intelligence, or the importance of creative play. These are topics we hear little about, yet they are no less important.

Each checklist is only a few hundred words long, the idea being to give you some starting points to which you can add your own ideas and experiences. After all, most of us are far too busy *being* parents to have the time to read endless chapters on the minutiae of toilet training. You'll probably dip in and out of this book when the mood strikes, or you have a specific question that needs answering – that's an ideal way to approach it.

Once you've finally worked your way through the book, you'll notice a similar approach to many of the issues. I'm a great believer in positive parenting. In other words, life will be infinitely easier and more pleasant for both you and your family if you start from the standpoint that parenting shouldn't be a battle. Effective parenting isn't about ruling through fear; you'll always have better relationships and behaviour if your child feels loved, valued and listened to.

When you become a parent you tend to look at your own childhood and family through fresh eyes. Only by being a mum myself have I fully learnt to understand the debt of gratitude that I owe to my own parents, who brought me up in a home filled with love, patience and enthusiasm. This book is for them.

Note: Children are referred to alternately as 'he' or 'she' from list to list.

Affection

Do you really need a book to tell you how to love your child? For most parents, feelings of warmth and affection come naturally – it's not something they have to think about. We instinctively know that children who grow up in a safe, happy environment go on to be well-adjusted, loving adults. Children who aren't so lucky, and grow up without parental affection, often end up troubled and dysfunctional. But it's not quite as straightforward as it sounds. The reality is that it's not enough just to love your child; it's *how* you love your child that will determine his or her future.

1   **Show affection.** Forget the old-school belief that showing affection won't prepare children for the harsh realities of life. Studies show that emotionally withdrawn families produce less confident, poorly adjusted adults.

2   **Give your time rather than toys.** How many parents assuage feelings of guilt about long working hours or family strife by showering their children with toys? Gifts are no substitute for genuine love and affection.

3   **Don't confuse laxity with love.** Children need rules and boundaries as much as they need affection. Over-indulgent parenting isn't the same as loving parenting (see page 43).

4   **Treat your children equally.** Boys, even when they are babies, tend to receive less physical affection from their parents than girls. Make a special effort to give boys and girls affection equally.

5   **Help your partner break old habits.** Dads often find expressing physical affection more awkward than

mums. Be patient – your partner may simply be reliving his childhood experience with his own father.

6 **Boost your child's self-esteem.** Children from families who regularly show physical affection to each other tend to enjoy better self-esteem and communication with their parents.

7 **Feel happier.** Hugging makes your body produce oxytocin, a 'feel-good' hormone. Research in the USA found that one 20-second hug a day makes children and parents happier and less stressed.

8 **Give unconditionally.** Try not to link every gesture of affection with something your child has done well, such as tidying her toys away or passing an exam. Impromptu hugs let your child know that your love is unconditional.

9 **'Look what I made!'** Children show their love in different ways, so don't worry if your child isn't always 'cuddly'. She may want to give you a painting she's done at school, or to share a bedtime story instead.

10 **'Aww Mum, gerroff!'** If your teen turns her nose up at the idea of a cuddle, try different gestures, such as a shoulder squeeze or hug from behind, both of which demonstrate affection without being too 'suffocating'.

Arguments

As soon as your child begins to develop his own personality and way of doing things, these will inevitably come into conflict with your own. With toddlers, this manifests itself as tantrums, which are dealt with later in this book (see page 165). With older children, who are able to express themselves more clearly, arguments arise when your boundaries and their wishes collide. Part of being a good parent is setting and maintaining reasonable boundaries (see page 43), but you also need to give your child the opportunity to air his grievances. Healthy parenting has no problem with setting the rules, but it's also about seeing your child's point of view. Use the following 10 tips to change a family argument from being destructive to productive.

1   **Stick to the point.** Focus on the issue in hand. Don't suddenly start bringing in other grievances or digging up past events.

2   **Is something else bothering you?** Make sure you're not just in the mood for a fight – hormones, tiredness, money worries, marital strife and work stress can all make you unusually irritable.

3   **Avoid sounding accusatory.** This means talking about 'I' not 'You'. For example, you could say, 'I felt disappointed when you...' rather than 'You disappointed me when...' It makes criticism feel less personal.

4   **Never say 'never'.** Try to avoid using absolutes, such as 'You never do your homework on time'. Absolutes are almost always not true and will make your child feel victimized. Keep to specific incidents.

5   **Don't gang up.** While it's important for parents to be in agreement, don't make your child feel as if she is being

mobbed. Avoid bringing in other people's opinions, such as those of teachers or other parents.

6 **Stay calm.** Tempers can soon escalate in an argument. Keep things cool by staying seated, breathing slowly and thinking carefully about what you want to say.

7 **Be nice.** Leave name-calling and hurtful comments to the playground. Verbal abuse – such as calling your child lazy, stupid or bad – has no place in a healthy home.

8 **Turn off the TV.** You can't have a sensible discussion if you're battling with noise from the television, phone or stereo. You need a quiet room where you're not going to be distracted or constantly interrupted.

9 **Learn to listen.** Children switch off when they feel a lecture coming on. Don't hog the conversation, talk over or interrupt. Use the 'Communication' checklist on page 25 to increase your listening skills and your child will want to open up to you.

10 **Manage your anger.** This may be a discussion, but you are the adult. Recognize when things are getting heated and be responsible enough to take time out.

Babysitters

We all need a night off from time to time. Professional childcare can be expensive, so parents often call on the services of an informal babysitter. Babysitters don't have to have any qualifications to look after your child, but you need to be as rigorous in your selection as you would be with any other form of childcare. This quick 10-point plan will help you sift the good from the bad, leaving you to enjoy a well-deserved break in confidence.

1　**When not to leave a child at home alone.** The NSPCC recommends that children under 13 should not be left at home alone, even for short periods of time. The law doesn't actually specify an age when a child can be left at home alone, but parents are committing an offence if leaving the child puts him or her at risk.

2　**Know the law.** The NSPCC suggests that babysitters should be aged 16 or over. If parents leave their child with a babysitter who is under 16, they could face possible neglect charges if anything goes wrong in their absence. Remember that some 16-year-olds may not be mature enough to handle responsibility.

3　**Get references.** Ask the sitter for at least two current references and make sure you follow them up. Personal recommendations are often a good idea.

4　**Where and when.** Tell your babysitter where you're going and when you'll be back. Don't deviate from these plans. Come back on time.

5　**Provide emergency contacts.** Make sure your babysitter knows basic first aid and has a list of emergency contacts, including mobile and landline numbers. Give your babysitter the details of a neighbour to contact if she needs help.

6 **'I don't like her.'** Make sure your child gets on with her carer. Never leave her with a babysitter who makes her uncomfortable – take the time to find one she likes. Children have good instincts.

7 **Give her the tour.** Don't just run for the door. Take the time to show the babysitter where everything is, including the first aid kit and telephone. Explain the rules about bedtimes, favourite teddies, snacks, TV and so on.

8 **Set the boundaries.** Make sure your babysitter knows that she can't smoke in the house or consume alcohol while your child is in her care.

9 **Pay properly.** A reliable, experienced babysitter is worth her weight in gold. Be prepared to pay around £5–£8 an hour.

10 **Consider a childminder.** If you want someone more qualified, www.surestart.gov.uk has a list of childminders in your area. Unlike babysitters, childminders must be registered and inspected by the Office for Standards in Education (Ofsted).

Bedrooms

Teenage bedrooms – yuk! You'll be familiar with clothes strewn everywhere, week-old mugs of tea and a carpet covered in magazines, books and CDs. It's enough to make any parent want to pull their hair out, but just how much say should we have in our children's space? The fact of the matter is that battles over bedrooms aren't really about cleanliness – they're about boundaries. Or at least they are for children. Your teenager is attempting to assert some independence and control over his surroundings. You're simply annoyed because his room smells of old socks. So where's a happy medium?

1 **Respect his space.** I hate to say it, but your child does need his own private space (see page 117). Children, especially teenagers, are intensely private at times and need a safe haven where they can express themselves without fear of ridicule.

2 **Don't go snooping.** Your teenager will never forgive you if you go poking around in his bedroom, especially if you find something embarrassing. And don't barge into your child's room if the door is closed. Respect his privacy – knock and wait for an answer.

3 **Reach a compromise.** Your child has to meet you half way. If he wants his clothes washed, for example, then he must put them in the laundry. If he wants his carpet vacuumed, he must clear the floor for you. If he wants his washing-up done, he takes his cups to the kitchen.

4 **Help him to create his space.** Encourage your child to take pride in his bedroom by paying for a room makeover. Get him to choose the colours and furniture within a set budget, and to design the scheme himself.

5 **Help him to stay tidy.** Children collect stuff by the bucketload. Encourage them to keep it out of the way by providing lots of storage. Under-bed drawers, blanket chests, stacking boxes, cupboard tidies – all these can help reduce a rubbish-strewn floor.

6 **Take heart.** Remember what you were like. Controlling their bedroom is a way for teenagers to assert their individuality and to be rebellious in a safe way. Most teens don't stay messy forever.

7 **Allow a lock on the door?** Lots of teenagers ask for a lock. Most just want to ensure they can get changed in peace or have a break from nosy siblings. Rather than a lock that needs a key – which could be a hazard in an emergency – you could agree to a catch on the door.

8 **Keep a distance.** If your house has the space, consider placing your teen's bedroom away from adult sleeping spaces. Attic or basement rooms allow privacy and peace all round.

9 **Set an example.** You can't expect your child to keep a clean bedroom if the rest of the house is a tip.

10 **Create a contract.** Children who are given respect and trust as emerging young adults tend to behave more responsibly than children who have their every move monitored. Nonetheless, make sure your child knows that the rules on smoking, sex and drugs extend to his bedroom. Mutual trust works both ways.

Bedwetting

Enuresis, the medical term for bedwetting, is incredibly common and affects over half a million children between the ages of six and 16. Unfortunately, both children and parents are embarrassed by it and fail to seek the help they need. Not only does this prolong the problem – bedwetting only clears up without treatment in around one in six children – it can also affect a child's confidence and social development. Children who wet the bed have been shown to suffer from lower self-esteem and feel isolated from their peers. With a little intervention, however, it's a problem that can soon be tackled.

1   **Is there a problem?** Bedwetting isn't considered a medical problem unless it continues after the age of five. Most children are dry at night by the age of three or four, but there can be a huge variation in the age at which this is achieved, even within the same family.

2   **Remember it's not deliberate.** Children who wet the bed are not doing it for attention or to be 'difficult'. There are numerous medical and psychological reasons behind bedwetting.

3   **Chat to your GP.** Some children find it difficult to wake up, even if their bladder is full. Others produce too much urine at night. Temporary conditions, such as a urine infection, can also cause bedwetting. Your family doctor should be your first port of call.

4   **Is stress playing a part?** Family strife, bullying, mental or physical abuse, school worries – all sorts of crises can trigger bedwetting. If there's no apparent medical explanation, could something be upsetting your child? This is especially true if a previously 'dry' child suddenly starts wetting the bed.

5 **Offer reassurance.** Don't punish or humiliate your child. Explain that it's a very common condition and that you'll try to sort it out together.

6 **Take practical steps.** Buy a waterproof mattress cover, leave the bathroom light on at night so that your child can find it easily, and always have spare nightclothes and bedding to hand in case she has an accident. Older children may want to change their pyjamas and bedclothes themselves.

7 **Help your child to make some changes.** Encourage your child to drink during the day instead of late in the evening; to wee twice before bedtime; and to cut out tea, coffee and cola (the caffeine these drinks contain is a diuretic, which makes your child's kidneys produce more urine).

8 **Consider an alarm.** An enuresis alarm, which can ring or vibrate when the first drop of urine hits the mattress, helps train your child into getting up at night to wee. Success usually takes about three months, but it's currently the most effective form of treatment.

9 **Consider medical help.** Desmopressin can be prescribed by your GP. It usually comes as a nasal spray or tablet, and works by slowing the production of urine overnight. Success rates are about 70 per cent, but the effects are usually immediate.

10 **Find support.** ERIC Online (Education and Resources for Improving Childhood Continence) has a wonderful website at www.enuresis.org.uk and a helpline (0845 370 8008) to help you stay positive.

Bereavement

Lots of children are lucky enough to get through their childhood without losing anyone significant, but a surprising number of young people experience the loss of a parent, grandparent, sibling or carer. The good news is that children are remarkably resilient, given the right love and guidance.

Cruse, the bereavement charity, has a fantastic website for anyone experiencing grief or supporting someone through a loss (www.crusebereavementcare.org.uk). Here is its list of some of the most common feelings that children experience when someone dies.

1   **'When is he coming back?'** Whatever your age, it can take a long time to believe that someone who matters very much to you is not coming back.

2   **'Why did it have to happen?'** Explanations are very important, but children may need to ask the same questions over and over again. It will take them time to accept what has happened, and the death may seem very unfair. They may be very angry that someone they care about has left them.

3   **'It was my fault.'** However far-fetched this may seem to you, many children worry that something they said or did, or didn't say or do, caused the death.

4   **'Will you die too?'** It is difficult for children to understand why someone dies, and they may become frightened about their own death or worry that someone else close to them will die soon.

5   **'Where has he gone?'** Younger children may find it more difficult to grasp that a dead person is not coming back and may ask repeatedly, 'Where has he gone?' expecting to be told of a place that they know about.

6 **'I wish I was dead.'** Like adults, children may sometimes feel it is not worth living without someone they love. They might imagine that if they die, they will be reunited with the dead person, or that the dead person will come back to life.

7 **'What happens to his body?'** Young children may need help to understand that when someone is dead the body no longer works and must be buried or burnt.

8 **'Will it hurt her when she is burnt?'** Children may think that being dead is like sleeping. They may need to be told there is no feeling or pain after death.

9 **'Who can I talk to?'** If talking to someone they know seems too big a step, it might be easier for them to talk to someone whose job it is to listen. Children can ring Cruse's free helpline number on 0808 808 1677 to chat to a trained adviser.

10 **'When will I feel better?'** Feelings tend to come and go in circles, and some people worry that they're feeling sad again, or angry, or guilty, when they thought they'd got over that feeling. What most children find, though, is that gradually, over time, things do get easier.

Budgeting for family life

Raising children is an expensive business. Current figures suggest that the cost of bringing up a child from birth to adulthood, including going to university, has now crashed through the £160,000 barrier (£280,000 if you send your child to private school). This breaks down to around £8000 a year, £650 a month or £20 a day, just to cover the essentials. On top of this, your ability to earn may have been reduced if one person needs to stay at home and look after the family. So how can you budget for family life, and are there any simple ways to make your money stretch further?

1 **Know your outgoings.** There's no mystery about saving money. Simply spend less than you earn. To do this, however, you need a clear picture of your finances. Log all your incomings and outgoings for a two-month period to give you a realistic snapshot.

2 **Ditch the luxuries.** If you want to reduce your outgoings, start with the non-essentials, such as satellite TV packages, magazine subscriptions, eating out, take-aways, mobile phones, additional cars and cosmetics.

3 **Reduce your food bills.** Buy in bulk, choose own-brand labels, and make the most of special offers. You can also save by buying directly from source, at farm shops, allotments and farmers' markets. Families on certain benefits can also get free fruit, vegetables, milk and vitamin vouchers at www.healthystart.nhs.uk.

4 **Pay off debts.** Credit is expensive, so paying off your debts is one of the best ways to boost your family's budget in the long term. Swap store cards and credit cards on to lower-rate loans and talk to your bank about drawing up a manageable repayment plan.

5 **Reassess your mortgage.** A mortgage is most people's biggest outgoing, yet few of us shop around for the best deal. The market is competitive, so talk to an independent mortgage adviser about swapping to a better deal – it could free up hundreds of pounds a year.

6 **Be a saver surfer.** Use the internet to shave money off your utility bills and insurance. Price comparison sites (such as www.moneysupermarket.com) can help you make big savings. Paying your bills by direct debit is also cheaper.

7 **Open savings accounts.** If you have yearly events that you need to save for – such as a family holiday or Christmas – open a savings account that you can't dip into. Set up regular payments and make sure access is restricted.

8 **Squirrel away any windfalls.** If you come into a lump sum, such as an inheritance, bonus or tax refund, don't be tempted to spend it. You won't have allowed for it in your family budget, so you won't miss it. Put it in a high-interest savings account for something really special.

9 **Get your child involved.** According to the Halifax Building Society, the average pocket money in the UK is £6.30 for 7–12-year-olds and £9.76 for 12–16-year-olds. Teach your child about budgeting for the things she wants. Open a bank account for her to help her save and earn interest.

10 **Claim what's due to you.** All families receive Child Benefit. You may also be entitled to other monies, such as a Sure Start Maternity Grant, Working Tax Credit and Child Tax Credit. For more information see www.direct.gov.uk.

Bullying

Bullying comes in many forms – emotional, physical or verbal – but the consequences are always devastating for the child involved. Left unchecked, persistent bullying can leave a child feeling depressed, withdrawn, nervous and isolated. School work and attendance often suffer, and at its very worst bullying can make a child feel suicidal. If you suspect your child is being bullied, you have a duty to tackle it – forget notions that bullying is somehow 'character-building' or just 'children being children'. It's not. Below you'll find 10 anti-bullying tips from Kidscape, the first charity in the UK established specifically to prevent bullying. Children, teachers and parents will also find lots more anti-bullying information on its website (www.kidscape.org.uk).

1 **Talk to your child**. If you are worried that your child is being bullied, ask him directly.

2 **Look out for signs and symptoms.** These include being frightened of getting to and from school, feeling 'ill' in the mornings, truanting, doing poorly in school work, becoming withdrawn, continually 'losing' pocket money or possessions, and unexplained bruises, cuts and scratches.

3 **Keep a written diary.** Take bullying seriously and find out the facts when told about an incident of bullying. Write everything in a notebook.

4 **Don't collude.** Never agree to keep the bullying a secret.

5 **Liaise with the school.** If the bullying is happening at school, talk to a teacher or the head teacher. Suggest a Kidscape programme in the school, or talk to the parent governors about drafting a school policy on bullying.

6 **Develop coping mechanisms.** Help your child to practise strategies such as shouting 'No', walking with confidence and running away.

7 **Don't allow bottling it up.** Give your child a chance to vent his feelings about being bullied.

8 **Go there in person.** Accompany your child if the bullying is happening on the way to or from school. Alternatively, ask that the bullies be kept at school until everyone has had a chance to get home.

9 **Consider self-defence classes.** If you feel it would help your child's confidence, ask him if he would like to take self-defence classes.

10 **Encourage socializing.** Invite children over to help your child make friends.

Career choices

When you are a child your options seem limitless. You can dream of being whatever you want to be, whether it's a pop star or a politician. Unfortunately, by the time school ends, most children find that their choices have become extremely limited. While good grades are important, the keys to finding the job you want are talking to people in the know, getting hands-on experience, and having the right set of personality traits. As a parent, you can play a vital role in helping your child to explore career choices – even as early as primary school. The objective isn't to push your child into any particular career, but to help her explore all the options, gain relevant skills and plan ahead.

1 **Take her seriously.** Even if you think your child is being unrealistic, try not to squash a dream she has about a particular career. Encourage her to find out more about what the job involves. Be enthusiastic.

2 **Help your child find out more.** Suggest that your child finds out more about the path she needs to follow to reach a particular goal. Will she need specific qualifications, or is work experience more important?

3 **Find inspiration.** People who have 'made it' can be very exciting to talk to, giving your child a first-hand account of what it took to achieve an ambition. Autobiographies can also be very inspirational.

4 **Network.** Use any contacts you or your friends may have to help your child meet the right people. Don't be afraid to call in favours.

5 **Gain work experience.** There's no substitute for hands-on experience. Encourage your child to find a work placement or job shadow. Just make sure she isn't being exploited as 'free labour'.

6 **Encourage summer jobs or part-time work.** For older children, part-time or freelance work is often a good route into a full-time occupation.

7 **Read all about it.** There are some excellent career guides for young people. Try Radio 1's ONELife webpages at www.bbc.co.uk/radio1/onelife or www. connexions-direct.com.

8 **Develop work skills.** Encourage your child to learn and demonstrate essential career skills, such as reliability, adaptability, punctuality, calmness, organization and time-management.

9 **Be a positive role model.** Too many children learn that work is a chore based on what they hear at home. Children of parents who enjoy their jobs tend to find great career satisfaction themselves.

10 **Talk to careers advisers.** If your child has access to a school careers adviser, make the most of it. He or she will have the latest job information and could help your child to find a work placement.

Choosing a school

Most parents want the best for their children, and part of that includes giving them a good education. Unless you can afford private school fees, however, you must choose between a handful of primary and secondary schools in your local authority. Well-regarded state schools tend to be over-subscribed, so it's vital that you start thinking about the options well in advance. It's one of the most important decisions you'll make as a parent.

1 **Do your homework.** Find out which schools are in your area. You can search for primary and secondary schools online in the Education and Learning section at www.direct.gov.uk. Your local authority will also have a list of local schools.

2 **Talk to your child.** Does your child have a preference? Where are his peers going? This is especially important for children moving from primary to secondary school.

3 **Establish any special requirements.** Gifted and very bright children, or children with specific learning difficulties, health issues and behavioural patterns may need a special school that can give them the support they need.

4 **Dig deeper.** Once you get an idea of the schools near you, investigate them in greater detail. This could include a visit in person, reading the school's inspection report at www.ofsted.gov.uk, and looking at the school's prospectus.

5 **Talk to other families.** Chat to parents and children about their experiences of a particular school. Children often pick up on problems – for example, bullying – that schools try to hide.

6 **Check the admissions policy.** Often you have a better chance of a successful application if you already have a child at the school, you are in the right catchment area, or your child's primary school is a feeder school to the secondary.

7 **Narrow down the options.** Local authorities vary, but you can usually apply to one or more primary schools and at least three secondary schools.

8 **Don't delay.** Don't miss the admissions deadlines: check the dates with your local authority. You will usually need to apply for a primary school place well before your child reaches the age of five. The deadline for secondary schools is usually in the autumn preceding the September your child is due to start.

9 **Lodge an appeal.** If your application is unsuccessful, you have a legal right to appeal. You will find details of how to make an appeal in the local authority's admission letter outlining your offer.

10 **If you choose a private school.** Independent schools have their own admissions policies, and many require you to apply months, if not years, in advance. Find out more from the Independent Schools Council (www.isc.co.uk).

Chores

There's no denying it – housework is a chore. But that doesn't mean children shouldn't help around the house. Every family member must chip in if the household is to run smoothly. Chores also help children to learn life skills, such as tidiness, responsibility, commitment and cooperation. The trick is to know which jobs are suitable for which age group, and how to motivate children when they can't face getting their hands dirty.

1 **Start young.** Toddlers love to help out. Make the most of this by giving young children household responsibilities. Start with small tasks, such as getting your child to clear away her toys. As she gets older, you can give her more complex tasks.

2 **Demonstrate.** Show your child what each specific chore involves, breaking it down into its component parts. For an older child, you might want to write down a list of the different stages, for example: 'Tidy bedroom = Clear up, dust the surfaces, change sheets and vacuum'.

3 **Take one step at a time.** It can be confusing, especially for young children, to learn more than one thing at a time. Teach one chore – such as how to put away clothes – and let her perfect that before you introduce another.

4 **Explain.** Children may wonder why they have to do chores. Explain that it's important for the whole family to pitch in to make things run smoothly. Once the chores are completed, it means the whole family can get on with having fun together.

5 **Don't look over her shoulder.** While very young children need constant monitoring and help, older

children should be left to do their chores in peace. This demonstrates trust in their competence and mutual respect.

6 **Start inspirational charts.** Set up a reward chart, stick it in a prominent position and add points for each task completed. Trade points for a non-material reward, such as a trip to the cinema or having a friend round for tea, but allow older children to earn extra pocket money for chores above and beyond what they usually do.

7 **Give lots of praise.** Children love to be told they've done well. Even if it's a chore your child has done a thousand times, don't forget to thank her and tell her what a wonderful job she's done.

8 **Don't do it yourself.** If you give in and do the chore yourself, your child will soon learn that Mum or Dad will pick up the slack. If your child refuses to do her allotted chore, make it clear that there are consequences.

9 **Implement logical consequences.** Parents shouldn't have to resort to threats. Make the point calmly that if your child does not do her chore, she will have a privilege removed or won't earn her desired reward.

10 **Balance it out.** Research shows that even in this day and age girls end up doing more chores than boys. Make sure both sexes are chipping in equally.

Common health problems

Here's a quick guide to 10 of the most common health problems in children, including notes about treatment. Always talk to your GP if your child is ill: it's better to be safe than sorry.

1 **Allergies.** These are extreme reactions by the immune system to usually harmless substances. Common allergies, such as hay fever and eczema, can develop for a number of reasons – environmental and genetic – so it's important to establish where the irritation is coming from. Ask your GP to refer your child to a specialist allergy clinic.

2 **Asthma.** Symptoms include shortness of breath, wheezing and a recurrent cough. The causes can be both environmental and genetic, but common triggers include house dust, pollen and cigarette smoke. Chest x-rays and lung function tests help with diagnosis, while treatment usually involves lifestyle changes and medication.

3 **Chickenpox.** This virus, which most children catch before the age of 10, is spread in droplets inhaled into the respiratory tract. It usually results in mild fever, headaches and itchy red spots. Paracetamol can relieve the fever, while calamine lotion and antihistamines will help combat the itching.

4 **Colds and flu.** Hundreds of different viruses cause colds and flu, which explains why children can be repeatedly ill. A cold usually causes mild symptoms, including a runny nose, sneezing and a sore throat. Flu is more severe and long lasting. Rest, paracetamol and plenty of fluids will be the usual treatment.

5 **Diarrhoea and constipation.** Dehydration, stress, a change in diet, or a gut infection can often upset

digestion. The occasional bout is nothing to worry about, but recurrences may indicate an underlying medical problem that needs attention. If the condition persists, or your child seems unwell, see your doctor.

6 **Earache.** This is most commonly caused by a viral or bacterial infection. Your GP can look inside your child's ear to establish the cause of the pain, and will usually suggest painkillers or antibiotics.

7 **Fever.** Any temperature above 37.2°C is classed as a fever. It's usually a sign of other problems, such as an infection or inflammation. Remove layers of clothing and gently sponge your child's skin with lukewarm water. Offer her plenty of fluids and give paracetamol to reduce the temperature. Seek medical help if the fever is above 38°C or there are other worrying symptoms, such as drowsiness, a rash, stiff neck or difficulty breathing.

8 **Glandular fever.** This is a virus passed in saliva. Signs include high fever, sore throat, lack of energy, swollen glands and muscle ache. A blood test will confirm a diagnosis, and treatment usually consists of paracetamol, fluids and rest. For a few children the infection leads to chronic fatigue syndrome. If your child seems continually tired weeks after the illness, talk to your GP.

9 **Headlice.** These are flat insects that live in hair. They spread easily from child to child, and can result in itching and tiny red spots on the scalp. Headlice like any type of hair, clean or dirty. Treat an infestation with an electrically charged comb or a medicated headlice shampoo.

10 **Vomiting.** Lots of things can cause vomiting, including tummy bugs, food intolerances and travel sickness. If it persists or your child has a fever, rash, diarrhoea, headache, abdominal pain or drowsiness, seek medical advice.

Communication

There are lots of reasons why you need to communicate with your child, whatever his age. Good communication enables parents and children to understand and support each other properly, express their needs, and discuss issues that matter. Being a good communicator also helps you to guide your child through any problems he may have, and to teach him about the big wide world. But good communication doesn't always come naturally, so here are 10 top tips to help smooth the way.

1 **Make it a two-way process.** Being a good communicator isn't the same as being a good talker. Listening is just as important. Let your child have equal space in the conversation.

2 **Use reflective listening.** This is about empathizing with your child, identifying his feelings and feeding it back. For example, 'You must have felt really upset when the teacher said that.'

3 **Don't ridicule.** Your child doesn't have the same vault of knowledge and experience that you have to draw from. That doesn't mean his ideas and feelings are stupid or silly. Take what he says seriously.

4 **Use open questions.** Phrases such as 'What do you think about...' invite more detailed responses than questions that can only be answered with 'Yes', 'No' or 'Don't know'.

5 **Watch your body language.** Your gestures will say as much as your mouth. Avoid aggressive body language, such as arm-crossing, pointing and standing over your child.

6 **Ensure understanding.** Make sure you've understood each other. To avoid misunderstanding, restate the

other person's position in your own words. 'So you're saying that you are really angry about...'

7 **Use age-appropriate language.** Use over-complex words and metaphors and your meaning will be lost. Use 'baby' language and you risk offending and alienating your child.

8 **Keep the lines of communication open.** Make it clear to your child that he can talk to you about anything, whether it's dating or bullying. You can't promise to agree, but you'll always be a good sounding board.

9 **Share, don't burden.** While talking about how you feel encourages your child to share his thoughts, there are some things parents shouldn't talk to their children about. Don't burden him with adult problems – such as marital or money worries – and don't expect him to prop you up emotionally.

10 **Don't stop!** Just like any skill, good communication needs constant practice. Spend lots of time talking, listening and sharing, even if there aren't any issues. That way, if a problem does arise, your child will find it easier to start a dialogue.

Computers and the internet

Love them or loathe them, computers and the internet have transformed our lives. In particular, they've had an enormous impact on children and their leisure time. And while the internet is an enormously positive educational and social resource, parents have a duty to check (just as they would with any other pastime) that their children aren't putting themselves in danger. Your child will probably be more cyber-smart than you, but just in case, here are some pointers from NCH (formerly known as the National Children's Home charity – www.nch.org.uk). They're aimed at children, so the best thing to do is to go through these points together.

1. **Keep the peace.** Always check that your parent is happy for you to enter a chatroom.

2. **Don't dish it out.** When you visit a chatroom it's a good idea to sign on using a nickname; and when you're chatting, don't give out your real name, your email address, your age, your phone number, where you live, your school, or whether you are a boy or girl; also, don't publish or send out a picture of yourself.

3. **Check before signing up.** It's often the case that before you can join a chatroom in the first place, or do other things on the internet, you'll need to sign up online and give out some personal info, such as your name, address and telephone number. Before you do this, first ask your parent if it's OK.

4. **Wise up!** You can't always be sure it's only people of your age in a chatroom. Chat safely: it could be an adult winding you up or trying to trick you.

5. **Pop ya collar!** Leave a chatroom the moment anything worries you. Let your parent know what's up, and report

it to the chat service provider. Save any conversations that you think could prove someone has been bullying or harassing you.

6 **Call time on web wasters!** Report bad taste and bad attitude messages in chatrooms to your parent/carer and your internet service provider, or whoever runs the chatroom.

7 **Back up.** Never arrange to meet anyone in the real world who you only know online, unless your parent agrees and comes with you. In any circumstances, never arrange to meet at your online friend's house. Stay in a public place, such as a café or shopping centre: it's safer.

8 **It's everywhere.** The internet is no longer something you use only through your computer at school or at home. Some mobile phones and games consoles also provide internet access. You need to be careful however you log on.

9 **Read the warnings.** Keep clear of over-18 chatrooms, websites and other parts of the internet intended for adults. The warnings are for your protection, and adult sites can sometimes do serious damage to your phone bill.

10 **Keep mum!** All passwords you use on computers are PRIVATE. Keep them to yourself.

Confidence and self-esteem

What is it to be confident and have high self-esteem? It usually means we have a positive attitude towards ourselves and others. It also involves feeling sure of our own worth and abilities. Above all, people who feel happy about themselves feel in control of their lives. And this may be why so many children, teenagers in particular, struggle with confidence and self-esteem. Childhood is a mixed-up time, full of strange experiences and new challenges. For older children, adolescence also brings its own set of problems, such as sexual feelings, changes in appearance and the urge for independence. It's no wonder children feel unsure of themselves at times. As a supportive parent, there are lots of things you can do to boost your child's confidence and self-esteem. Here are 10 for starters.

1 **Set an example.** The family is the single biggest influence on a person's self-esteem. In particular, parents who demonstrate confidence and high self-esteem are best placed to nurture these traits in their children.

2 **Love, love, love.** Affection should never be conditional. Remember to tell your child how much you love her and how important she is to you.

3 **Listen with interest.** Self-esteem comes from feeling that your opinion matters. Take a genuine interest in what your child has to say.

4 **Treat her with respect.** Feeling good about yourself also comes from sensing that other people hold you in high regard. Treat your child with respect – whether it's taking her seriously, showing trust or giving her responsibility.

5 **Give your time.** What better way to show how much your child means to you than spending time with her?

You can reinforce this by finding an interest you can share together (see page 67).

6 **Make your child feel needed.** Children like to feel that their input is valuable. Let your child help you practically, ask her advice and solicit her opinion.

7 **Recognize your child's achievements.** A child whose achievements are never praised soon becomes demotivated. Sing your child's praises, however small the achievement. Make it specific; for example, 'You've chosen really nice colours for your picture', rather than just 'Well done'.

8 **Count all successes.** Many parents measure their child's success by academic achievement. This can be devastating for children whose talents lie elsewhere. Recognize the importance of all different sorts of skills, whether with sport, people, art or music.

9 **Try something completely different.** Confidence comes from having the courage to try new, challenging things. Encourage your child to set new goals, try new foods, make new friends, play new sports and games, and tackle new subjects.

10 **Learn from mistakes.** Failure is an important part of the learning process. People with high self-esteem see it as an opportunity to learn something about themselves. Don't expect perfection; it doesn't exist.

Cosmetics

Ask 20 parents about their views on make-up and you'll get 20 different answers. It's a tricky subject to negotiate because it brings into play lots of different issues, such as independence, self-esteem, role models and sexuality. A recent survey by consumer analysts Mintel found that more than 60 per cent of primary school girls regularly wear make-up, and this went up to 90 per cent among 14-year-old girls. Some parents see it as harmless fun, while others worry about the pressure on young children to look grown up. Either way, here are a few tips to help you and your child come to some kind of compromise.

1 **Check school policy.** Most schools have a clear, sensible policy on make-up, so ensure your child follows their guidelines. Primary schools tend to ban it altogether, while secondary schools usually limit make-up to the minimum.

2 **Encourage good skin care.** Children often start to wear make-up during puberty, when hormones begin to wreak havoc on their skin and self-esteem. Encourage your child to practise a good skincare routine to improve her confidence. This goes for boys too.

3 **Understand media images.** Children and teenagers are susceptible to feelings of low self-esteem because they cannot measure up to the airbrushed perfection they see in magazines and on TV. Make sure they know the difference.

4 **Improve self-esteem.** Your child shouldn't learn to base her self-esteem on her looks. Use the 'Confidence and self-esteem' checklist on page 29 to help her create a positive self-image.

5 **Set an example.** It's difficult to say 'No' to your teen if you are wearing lots of make-up yourself.

6   **Suggest natural cosmetics.** Most cosmetics contain a large amount of synthetic substances, many of which are potentially irritating to young skin. Stick to chemical-free, natural brands.

7   **Suit the occasion.** Make-up often forms the basis for many a slumber party or girlie get-together. Let your child experiment with make-up, but make it clear that what she can wear inside the house is not the same as for out and about.

8   **Buy a book.** If they're going to do it, at least help them do it properly. *The 21st Century Beauty Bible* by Sarah Stacey and Josephine Fairley, and *Perfect Make-up Ooh La La* by Susie Galvez are both excellent guides to make-up for teens.

9   **Don't make fun.** However ridiculous your child looks while experimenting with make-up, be careful not to make hurtful comments. Most teens don't feel happy with how they look, so it's important not to make things worse.

10   **Talk to a dermatologist.** If your child is wearing make-up to hide bad skin, ask if she'd like to talk to a dermatologist (see page 179).

Creativity

Being creative isn't just being able to paint or draw – it's a way of thinking. Creativity is the ability to see things in a new way, to solve problems by coming up with exciting, novel solutions. Much of the education our children receive focuses on what's called 'convergent thinking', the ability to come up with a single correct answer to a question. Creativity, however, involves 'divergent thinking', the ability to come up with lots of different, unusual solutions to a problem – a skill that will be endlessly useful during their adult life. But how can you encourage your child to be creative in his everyday life?

1   **Provide the right environment.** Encourage your child to behave in as many different creative ways as possible by providing a variety of stimulating materials, such as art supplies, fabrics, musical instruments, books, dressing-up clothes and other creative props.

2   **Don't be too prescriptive.** Children whose creative play is constantly controlled by a parent lose the joy and spontaneity that come from discovering things for themselves.

3   **Avoid 'wrong' answers.** Creativity isn't about right or wrong answers. The greatest discoveries are always found when people think 'outside the box'. Allow your child to do the same.

4   **Try new things.** Children should learn that 'different' doesn't necessarily mean better or worse. Expose your child to different cultures and experiences, whether travel, food, cultures, clothes or accents.

5   **Pretend to be 'King for a Day'.** Get your child to imagine he rules the world. What would he change? Who would live in his castle? What would he ban or make

compulsory? This game isn't just wishful thinking; it's about creating goals and dreams.

6 **Play 'What if?'** Pose questions that encourage your child to think about possible scenarios and forward planning. What if it snowed every day? What if cars disappeared? What if we lived under the sea?

7 **Take a prop.** Choose one household item and ask, 'In how many different ways could this object be used?' A colander, for example, could also be a hat, a seat for teddy, a fruit bowl, a drum – the more obscure the idea the better!

8 **Enjoy story time.** Acting out stories, playing different roles and using puppets encourages children to create different endings to the same scenarios. Can your child help the characters to have a happy ending?

9 **Let's pretend.** Imagining yourself as a creature or object helps you to think and behave differently. Get your child to mimic how the animal or object acts and moves. Switch between loud and quiet objects, fast and slow, and so on.

10 **Change roles.** Putting themselves in someone else's shoes is a great way for children to develop empathy and explore their feelings. Look at pictures of people in different situations and ask your child how he thinks each person feels.

Crime and anti-social behaviour

Read the tabloids and you'd get the idea that practically every teenager is involved in crime or anti-social behaviour. The reality is that youth crime is actually decreasing, and of the crime that does take place, most is non-violent and 'petty', such as shoplifting, vandalism and under-age drinking. If your child does get into trouble with the police, however, it can be a distressing experience for the whole family. The good news is that the juvenile justice system is designed to nip crime in the bud rather than to lock up children, so here's what you can expect from the process.

1   **Age and the law.** If your child is under 10 years old, she cannot be charged with a criminal offence. Once she is 10 or over, she will be dealt with by the Youth Justice System.

2   **The police station.** If a child is detained at a police station, the parents must automatically be informed. If a parent cannot be present, another adult, such as a social worker or other responsible person, can stand in.

3   **Right to representation.** Your child has the right to obtain legal advice. If your family does not have a solicitor, one will be provided. This is free to everyone under 17 years of age.

4   **Detention.** The police should not detain your child for more than 24 hours without charging her, unless an officer with the rank of superintendent (or above) or a magistrate gives permission.

5   **Reprimand.** For a minor first offence, the police will probably issue a reprimand (formerly called a caution). This is usually enough to prevent most children reoffending.

6 **Final Warning.** This is issued by the police for a second offence, no matter how minor. It is also possible to get a Final Warning if a first offence is too serious for a Reprimand.

7 **Youth Offending Team.** If your child has received a Reprimand or Final Warning, she will be referred to a Youth Offending Team (YOT). They will talk to you and your child about the offence and how she might avoid further offending.

8 **Youth court.** For very serious offences your child may have to attend a youth court. This is designed to be less intimidating than an adult court; parents can sit close to their children, and the court uses language a young person can understand.

9 **Penalties.** If your child is found guilty, magistrates have a range of penalties to choose from, including a compensation order (when compensation is paid to the victim), a referral order (which involves working with a youth offender panel to prevent further offending), a community sentence (such as electronic tagging), or a custodial sentence.

10 **Criminal records.** The law recognizes that young offenders are special cases, so their criminal records are wiped clean once they reach 18 years of age.

Depression

Depression isn't always easy to spot in children, as they often lack the ability to express their feelings. A young person who is depressed may have a continually low mood, feelings of inadequacy, overwhelming guilt or anxiety, or irrational thoughts. Depression can also manifest itself in other less obvious ways, such as self-harm, eating disorders and even bullying (see pages 139, 47 and 15). At its worst, depression may lead to suicidal thoughts and behaviour, so it's really important to get help if you are worried about your child.

1 **Spot the signs.** Is your child's behaviour different from normal? Toddlers might be excessively tearful or clingy, have trouble sleeping or eating, or wet the bed. Older children can lose interest in school or friends, become irritable and rowdy, uncommunicative, withdrawn or isolated, and stop taking care of themselves.

2 **Take it seriously.** Left untreated, depression can have a lasting impact on a child's self-esteem, academic success and social development. Tackle it now.

3 **Talk to your child.** Try to get him to talk about his feelings. Don't be disheartened if he is initially hostile; depressed people often refuse to accept that there's anything wrong. Trust your instincts as a parent. Use the 'Communication' checklist on page 25 to help.

4 **Talk to your GP.** Whether your child confides in you or not, you must talk to your doctor. Your GP will be able to suggest lots of different ways to help your child, including individual counselling, family therapy and creative therapies, such as drama or music.

5 **Take exercise.** Encourage your child to play a sport or get active. Physical exercise releases happy hormones,

such as serotonin, which combat depression, and also helps your child make new friends, get fit and feel good about himself.

6 **Avoid stimulants and sugar.** Sugar gives an instant energy rush, but this is followed by a sharp drop in energy an hour or so later, which can lead to a low mood. Caffeine, found in tea, coffee and cola, is also linked to anxiety and depression.

7 **Try mood-boosting foods.** Complex carbohydrates, such as brown rice, will help keep your child's mood stable. Foods that contain tryptophan – milk, lean meat and poultry – are thought to be calming, while essential fatty acids from oily fish help brain receptors with serotonin uptake. Wholegrains, bananas, asparagus, spinach, chickpeas and nuts are also well-known mood boosters.

8 **Build self-esteem.** Work on improving your child's self-esteem (see page 29).

9 **Look closer to home.** Could family life be contributing to your child's stress? Make sure that you're not piling on extra pressure with relationship problems, conflict, money worries and unrealistic expectations.

10 **Consider medication as a last resort.** For severe depression your GP may prescribe an antidepressant. This should only be given alongside counselling or psychotherapy, as a dual approach is both safer and more effective.

Diet and junk food

It's extremely important that your child eats healthily. Children not only rely on the energy and nutrients from food to help them grow, but poor nutrition can have a devastating effect on their life chances. Research has shown that children who eat a poorly balanced diet are at higher risk of developing learning problems, mood swings, hyperactivity, mental health issues, disturbed sleep and allergies. Not only that, but a bad diet in childhood is directly linked to serious health problems in adulthood, such as heart disease and cancer. So how can you create a healthy, balanced diet for your child?

1 **Include starchy foods.** These should make up a third of the food your child eats. Starchy foods are a great source of energy, nutrients, fibre, calcium, iron and B vitamins. Healthy choices include wholemeal bread, wholewheat pasta, brown rice and wholegrain breakfast cereals.

2 **Offer lots of fruit and veg.** The recommended minimum is five portions a day, and it's easy to work out. One portion is equal to one glass of fruit juice, a banana, seven strawberries, one tablespoon of sultanas, one slice of melon, one tomato or two broccoli spears.

3 **Make fish a part of the diet.** Fish is an excellent source of protein, vitamins and minerals. Your child should eat at least two portions per week, including one portion of omega-rich oily fish, such as salmon, mackerel or sardines. Children should avoid shark, swordfish or marlin because high levels of mercury in these fish can affect their developing nervous system.

4 **Build calcium levels with dairy foods.** Calcium is vital for the development of your child's bones and teeth. Great sources include milk, cheese, yoghurt, soya beans, tofu and nuts.

5 **Choose the right fats.** Go for unsaturated fats instead of saturated ones. This means opting for vegetable oils (such as sunflower or olive oil), oily fish, avocados, nuts and seeds instead of fat from meat, hard cheese, butter, lard and cream.

6 **Reduce salt intake.** Too much salt can raise your child's blood pressure, increasing the risk of her developing heart disease in later life. Children aged 1–3 should have no more than 2 grams of salt per day (1 teaspoon = 5 grams); ages 4–6 should have no more than 3 grams; 7–10s no more than 5 grams; and over-11s no more than 6 grams.

7 **Keep sugar intake low.** Too much sugar is linked to tooth decay and obesity. Research also suggests a link between excessive sugar consumption and mood swings. Avoid giving your child sugary drinks, frosted cereals and sweets on a daily basis.

8 **Check if vitamin supplements are necessary.** Children who eat a well-balanced diet should not need vitamin supplements. If your child is a picky eater or has dietary problems, however, talk to your GP, as children aged between six months and five years can sometimes need extra sources of vitamins A, C and D.

9 **Ditch the junk food.** Processed foods, such as take-aways, crisps, chips and biscuits tend to be higher in unhealthy fats, sugar and salt. Visit www.jamieoliver. com and download free recipes designed to tempt young palates away from junk food.

10 **Ask for help.** If you're still struggling to get your child to eat well, you can find advice on www.eatwell.gov.uk, or talk to your GP. Families on a low budget may also be entitled to free fruit, vegetables, milk and vitamin vouchers (see www.healthystart.nhs.uk).

Disability

Caring for a disabled child comes with its own set of rewards and challenges. While most parents of disabled children soon become experts in their child's condition and how best to manage it, this doesn't stop the job of caring being lonely and frustrating at times. Looking after a disabled child can increase the emotional and physical strain on parents, while children with disabilities need specific support and guidance as they grow into adults. So what can you do, and what help are you and your family entitled to?

1 **Contact Social Services.** Your local Social Services department may provide practical help and support for your child and you as a family, including short breaks, nursery provision, aids and equipment, and home help. Many local authorities also have specific teams for children with disabilities.

2 **Draw on the Health Service.** The NHS should cover all aspects of your child's healthcare. Your GP will probably be your first point of contact, but he can refer you to other health services, such as health visitors, mobility aids, speech therapists or physiotherapists.

3 **Talk to your Local Education Authority.** Your child is entitled to the best education possible. Your LEA can provide additional help and support for children who are assessed as having special educational needs (SEN).

4 **Find out about financial support.** There's a wide range of benefits you may be entitled to, including Disability Living Allowance, Carer's Allowance, Tax Credits, Income Support and Housing Benefit. Ask your Social Services department, or get in touch with the charity Contact a Family for advice on your entitlements (www.cafamily.org.uk) or freephone 0808 808 355).

5 **Find support groups.** These can offer information, practical help, contact with other parents, helplines or drop-in advice centres. To find organizations for people with specific disabilities, and to make contact with other carers, visit www.direct.gov.uk/en/CaringForSomeone.

6 **Contact Shared Care Network.** This national organization provides family-based short breaks for disabled children. It represents over 300 local schemes that link disabled children with people in the community who provide regular short-term care. Visit www.sharedcarenetwork.org.uk

7 **Discover the Early Support Programme.** This programme (www.earlysupport.org.uk) has lots of information and advice specially developed for families with very young disabled children (under-fives).

8 **Show your child Whizz-Children.** If your child has disabilities, he should check out www.whizz-kidz.org.uk. Their 'Kidz Zone' has a busy online message-board, events to join in, bags of information and real-life stories.

9 **Upgrade to *Ouch!*** Older children and teenagers with disabilities will love *Ouch!*, the BBC's sassy, cynical and very funny online magazine (www.bbc.co.uk/ouch). It's great for parents too.

10 **Find support for siblings.** Brothers and sisters of children with disabilities can often feel left out, guilty or worried. Sibs (www.sibs.org.uk) offers support and information for children growing up with a brother or sister with special needs, a disability or chronic illness.

Discipline and boundaries

In the same way that children find routines comforting, boundaries help your child feel secure. Far from being something that parents should shy away from, they help your child make sense of the world, teaching her what's acceptable behaviour and what isn't. Once you've set your boundaries, however, it's just as important to maintain them. That's where discipline comes in.

1. **Learn to set boundaries.** Don't be afraid to be clear about what your limits are when it comes to behaviour. You could even get your child to help you draw up a contract of 'house rules', including bedtimes, chores, behaviour and language.

2. **Use 'No' sparingly.** All parents need to say 'No', but make sure you don't find yourself saying it all the time or it will lose its impact. Try saying 'Let's do this instead' or 'Let's save that for later'.

3. **Avoid 'Because I said so'.** How many times have you heard yourself saying that? If possible, try to explain the reasons behind a decision; it helps your child understand that your rules aren't arbitrary.

4. **Expect children to test boundaries.** All families have arguments about boundaries – it's completely normal. Your child is growing and learning to think for herself. Conflict is a natural consequence of different points of view.

5. **Be flexible.** Your boundaries should change as your child gets older. Be open to compromise. Change the rules if the old boundary seems outdated: for example, bedtimes will get later as your child grows older.

6 **Be a grown-up.** Children don't need another best friend; they need a parent. Make sure you're not bending the rules just because you don't like making unpopular decisions.

7 **Benefit from positive parenting.** Use praise and encouragement, rather than negative punishment, to foster good behaviour . Children naturally want to please their parents, and research shows that smacking tends only to make bad behaviour worse.

8 **Control your anger.** Verbal attacks and angry outbursts will only make the situation worse, and leave your child feeling frightened and confused. Your message will also be lost in the middle of the maelstrom. Take time out if you need to.

9 **Make a reward board.** Stick the board on the wall and add points each time your child behaves well. Explain to her how it works. When she's got 10 or 20 points, trade those points for a mutually agreed reward. Don't take points away for bad behaviour, simply don't award any; that's incentive enough for a child.

10 **Learn how to praise.** Praising good behaviour encourages more of the same. You can learn how to do this on page 127.

Divorce and separation

It's always grim when parents go their separate ways, and it's particularly hard on the children. Everything gets thrown up into the air – finances, living arrangements and family dynamics – so it's not surprising that most families describe it as the most stressful thing they ever go through. That said, there are lots of things you can do to make the process as painless as possible.

1 **Don't pretend.** Don't make out that everything's fine. Children can smell a rat a mile off. If there are problems, it's best to be open. Divorce is hard enough without having to deal with it as a complete surprise. Honesty is a must.

2 **Be discreet.** Don't be indiscriminately open or involve your child in discussions meant for you and your partner. He just needs to know what's going on. For example: 'Mum and Dad are having some problems; it doesn't affect how we feel about you. We're working hard to sort them out, but one solution might be living apart.'

3 **Allow your child to grieve.** It can really hurt to hear how your divorce is affecting your child, but you have a responsibility to listen. Be understanding and allow him to vent his frustrations and worries. Don't be surprised if he has a mission to mend the marriage.

4 **It's not his fault.** Children often blame themselves, believing that if they'd just 'been better' none of this would have happened. Make absolutely sure that your child knows the divorce is not his fault.

5 **Don't create divisions.** Children can feel a conflict of loyalty between two warring parties. Don't ask your child to take sides. He will want to spend time with both his parents, regardless of who initiated the split.

6 **Expect different reactions.** Children will react differently depending on temperament and age. Very young children may show regressive behaviour, such as clinginess or bedwetting. School-age children may be able to vocalize their feelings more easily, but watch out for 'silent' problems, such as truancy, withdrawing or risky behaviour.

7 **Consider family therapy.** Mediation and other types of group therapy can help all members of the family express their feelings and move forwards. Ask your GP for your nearest family counsellor.

8 **Don't close the book.** Months or years down the line you and your partner may have moved on, but don't be surprised if your child hasn't. Allow him to bring up the subject if there are unresolved issues.

9 **Keep it civil.** Research shows that children come off worst when parents continue to argue over access. Never criticize your ex in front of your child, even if that person caused the split. Take care not to make your child a go-between; if you need to talk to your ex, do it yourself.

10 **Be optimistic.** However difficult things get, the situation *will* eventually settle down. A recent poll by www.insidedivorce.com found that 80 per cent of 10–15-year-olds were happy with their new family life, and the same number also said things were just as good or better since the separation.

Drugs

It's almost inevitable that your child will be given the opportunity to experiment with drugs at some stage. You can't wrap your child up in cotton wool, so how do you protect her from illegal substances, and what can you do if drugs become a problem?

1 **Get talking.** Encourage open and honest discussions about drugs right from the word go. Make sure your child knows she can come and talk to you, and explain your standpoint from the start. You could use a TV programme or news report about drugs to spark a conversation.

2 **Get your facts straight.** By the time your child is at secondary school, she'll probably know more about drugs than you. Arm yourself for informed discussions about everything from alcohol to category A substances.

3 **Boost self-esteem.** Children who have serious drug problems tend to be escaping from home life, school pressures or feelings of self-loathing. Use the 'Confidence and self-esteem' checklist on page 29 to ensure your child feels good about herself.

4 **Get the school involved.** Find out what your child's school is doing in terms of drugs education. Is it tackling the issues head on or trying to avoid them? See 'Liaising with school' on page 81 for help about getting involved with school policy.

5 **Set an example.** Are you a heavy drinker or smoker? Do you use cannabis or any other drug recreationally? Be sure that you're not sending mixed signals about drug use to your child.

6 **Don't panic.** If you think your child is using drugs, try to stay calm. Don't start talking about blame; just listen

to what she has to say before working out a plan of action.

7 **Show compassion.** Say that you sympathize and remember what peer pressure feels like. Encourage your child to share her feelings, but if she won't open up, maybe she'd prefer to talk to another adult or close friend?

8 **Be loving.** Remind her that your love is unconditional, and that even though you don't condone her behaviour, you will always help and support her as best you can.

9 **Get help.** Don't try to sort this out by yourself. Visit www.talktofrank.com or call the Talk to Frank drugs information helpline on 0800 77 66 00 – they'll put you in touch with local and national services that can provide counselling and treatment.

10 **Stay positive.** Remember that the majority of young people who try drugs do not go on to become problem users, especially if you seek help early on.

Eating disorders

There are two main types of eating disorder – anorexia and bulimia. People with anorexia attempt to keep their body weight unhealthily low by excessive dieting, vomiting or exercising. People with bulimia, on the other hand, are caught in a cycle of binge-eating large amounts of food and then purging themselves by vomiting, taking laxatives or fasting. Unlike anorexics, people with bulimia can often maintain a normal weight. The reasons behind someone developing an eating disorder are varied, but in general, eating disorders seem to develop slowly over time, and often coincide with periods of stress or insecurity, such as exams or a family break-up.

Caring for someone with an eating disorder is both upsetting and frustrating. Thankfully, both GPs and the wider healthcare community take anorexia and bulimia in children very seriously, and your first port of call should be the family doctor, even if your child refuses to be present. If necessary, a GP can refer the child to a mental health professional specializing in this area. Treatment may include dietary control, as well as individual and family therapy aimed at resolving underlying emotional problems. If your child continues to lose a great deal of weight, he or she may need to spend some time in hospital or a special unit, where treatment can be more closely monitored.

As well as medical help, family support is crucial. ChildLine, the children's charity, offers the following advice for parents who want to help their child overcome an eating disorder.

1   **Become a good listener.** Don't jump in feet first – listen carefully to what your child has to say.

2   **Don't overreact.** Talk about the disorder as calmly as possible. Give your child a chance to explain his or her point of view.

3 **Show patience.** You will need to be gentle but firm; it can take a long time for your child to want to change.

4 **Try to be consistent.** Parents especially must agree on their strategy and stick to it.

5 **Work together.** Communicate clearly with each other as a family and cooperate with health professionals.

6 **Expect denial.** People with eating disorders often refuse to believe that there is a problem, so you must be willing not to believe what you are told.

7 **Do your research.** Learn more about eating disorders from whatever sources you can find.

8 **Be encouraging.** Try to persuade your child to seek professional help.

9 **Know the limitations.** Accept that you can't force your child to stop the food-controlling behaviour; change has to come from the child, when he or she is ready.

10 **Understand.** It's important to know what you are dealing with. Remember that an eating disorder is comparable to an addiction.

Emotional intelligence

You might not have heard of the term 'emotional intelligence' or EI, but chances are you're already using it every day. It refers to the ability to understand your own feelings and those of people around you. Different types of emotional intelligence include empathy, sympathy, good manners, diplomacy, timing and sensitivity to the feelings of others. People with high levels of emotional intelligence find social interactions much easier. Since they understand themselves and the needs of others, they find it easier to make friends, handle conflict, solve personal problems and manage their own emotions. As a parent, it's really important to encourage these skills in your child. And, just like any other kind of skill, EI is something that can be improved with practice.

1   **Be a role model.** Your child watches you very closely. How do you respond to difficult feelings? How resilient are you? How aware of other people's feelings are you? How do you behave with your partner?

2   **Expand your child's vocabulary.** Toddlers may know only the words 'happy' and 'sad', but very soon your child will need the right words to talk about new feelings. Give her the verbal tools to express herself.

3   **Make emotions an everyday subject.** Emotions can be a useful daily topic of conversation. It doesn't have to be about how *you* are feeling; it could be about friends and other family members.

4   **Role-play emotions and feelings.** Young children love pretending. Encourage your child to play-act different emotions – excitement, fear, confusion – and talk about situations that might cause those feelings.

5   **Play 'Guess the Emotion'.** This exercise helps your child to read other people's feelings. Display the

outward characteristics of an emotion and let her guess
what it is. Make sure she knows it is just a game.

6 **Mix it up.** Children who socialize with people from all
different walks of life tend to have a more sophisticated
grasp of social relationships and dynamics. Let them
interact with people of all ages too – from babies to
grandparents.

7 **Don't overprotect.** It's tempting to wrap your child in
cotton wool, and parents often feel they should shield
their children from any type of emotional upset. Even
young children need to experience different emotions
and learn how to handle them.

8 **Embrace the cliché.** The central idea of EI is 'Treat
others the way you would want to be treated'. It's an
age-old idea, but one that children readily understand.

9 **Remember there are no 'bad' emotions.** Teach your
child that whatever emotion she's feeling, what matters
is how she *acts* on it. If your child feels guilty about
being mean to a friend, for example, explain that it's OK
to feel guilty, but that she needs to focus on resolving
the situation.

10 **Practise empathy.** In any kind of interaction with
other people, encourage your child to think 'What might
they be feeling?'. Everyone sees the world in a different
way. If your child can get a sense of what's going on
in other people's lives, she will find it much easier to
communicate with them.

Exams

Whatever you think of British education, you can't get around the fact that a large part of it is based on exams. Even small children are tested regularly, so it's important for parents to help children learn how to approach exams sensibly. Skills such as organized revision and time management are vital, but, more importantly, your job as a parent is to encourage your child to approach tests with the right attitude – calmly, confidently and with a sense of perspective.

1 **Know your child.** You might want your child to be a rocket scientist, but do you really know his favourite school subjects? Talk to the school well before examinations so that you have realistic expectations of your child's strengths and weaknesses.

2 **Do your homework.** It's helpful for parents to know when exams are imminent; the main ones are at Key Stage 1 (age seven), Key Stage 2 (age 11), Key Stage 3 (age 14), GCSEs (at 16), AS levels (at 17) and A levels (at 18). Find out more at www.parentscentre.gov.uk.

3 **Value non-academic skills.** Long gone are the days when exam grades determined a child's future. Good results will open doors, but other skills, such as creativity (see page 33) and emotional intelligence (see page 51), are just as important in adult life.

4 **Get organized.** Revision works best with a realistic plan, so encourage your child to work in manageable chunks, and suggest that he keeps to a timetable. Make sure he breaks up periods of study with relaxation.

5 **Create space to study.** How many children have to revise at the kitchen table? Your child needs a proper space to work; somewhere quiet, warm and well lit. Let

the rest of the family know how important the work is and that your child is not to be disturbed.

6 **Use the web.** Make use of online resources. There are some excellent websites, full of information about how to prepare well, cope with stress, what to do if things don't go to plan and much more. Try Radio 1's ONELife and GCSE Bitesize, both at www.bbc.co.uk.

7 **Don't pass it on.** Parents often get nervous at exam time, remembering how it was for them, and pass it on to their child. Remind yourself that your goal is to help your child get the skills and attitude to cope on his own, including dealing with setbacks.

8 **Be interested.** Find a low-key way of asking how revision is going and whether he's hit a problem. It can be a wonderful boost to your child's confidence and energy.

9 **Ensure your child is eating, sleeping and exercising.** It's much easier to cope with the exam stress if your child is getting enough sleep and eating sensibly. Encourage him to have a change of scenery or get some fresh air.

10 **Steps to take if it all goes wrong.** If your child doesn't do as well as expected, it's not the end of the road. Give him praise for what has been achieved, and talk about practical future steps. Look into alternative learning routes, such as coursework assessments. Talk to the school.

Exercise

Children are naturally bouncy and full of beans, so why is there such a problem getting them to exercise? The answer is complex. A rise in factors such as road traffic accidents and 'stranger danger' has put a lot of parents off letting their children walk or cycle alone. School sports and playing fields have been in a general decline thanks to funding problems. And, not surprisingly, televisions and computers have encouraged many children to lead a more sedentary life. There are lots of benefits to being physically active – from maintaining a healthy weight to improving your social life – so what can you do to get your child off the couch?

1 **Make it fun.** Which would you prefer – an hour's snowboarding or 60 minutes sweating on a treadmill? It's a no-brainer, so don't forget to make exercise fun for your child too. Think about exciting sports she'd like, such canoeing, rollerblading or surfing.

2 **Start early.** An active child is more likely to carry her fitness into adulthood, so get your child up and out of the house as soon as you can.

3 **Be a role model.** Your child will pick up on your enthusiasm, so make sure you're setting a good example. You don't need to be sporty – a boogie in the bedroom or an hour's gardening is just as good as a gruelling workout in the gym.

4 **Make tiny tweaks.** Children should be doing an hour's moderate exercise a day. It doesn't have to be taken in one go – a quick cycle to school or kick-about in the park and she'll soon make up the 60 minutes.

5 **Have family fun.** Get out as a family. Don't make it a miserable wet walk in the rain. Grab your cossies and

head for the local water park. Go 10-pin bowling, sailing or go-kart racing.

6 **Encourage fun with friends.** Teens may not want to hang around with their parents. *Soooooo* embarrassing. Suggest they organize a five-a-side football match with friends, or help them organize a day paint-balling.

7 **Consider active holidays.** Make holidays as active as term-time. Head for the mountains to go walking or skiing, or spend a summer splashing around in the sea.

8 **Benefit from outdoor pursuits.** Children who love the outdoors tend to be naturally more active. Being outside will also boost your child's sense of well-being, expand her horizons, and help her learn about the natural world.

9 **Join a club.** Sports clubs are a great way for your child to make friends, improve her social skills and get fit in a safe environment. Active Place (www.activeplaces.com) has a list of over 50,000 sport facilities in the UK.

10 **Pull the plug.** It can be difficult to pull your child away from the TV or computer. Make sure you have clear times in the day when technology is off-limits, and pull the plug if you have to.

Family outings

Whether you have a toddler or a teen, there are thousands of things you can do together as a family. From spooky castles to chocolate factories, Britain has them by the bucketload. To make the day a success, remember to plan ahead, book tickets in advance if possible, and work out the journey. For tried-and-tested family outings check out www.daysoutwithchildren. co.uk or www.raring2go.co.uk. In the meantime, here are some pointers to get you started.

1   **Bring history to life.** Ruined castles, dungeons, archaeological digs, historical re-enactments, battles, Victorian classrooms – take your child back to the past and you'll reignite his imagination.

2   **Find the life aquatic.** Water parks, the seaside, swimming pools, canal barges, maritime museums, tall ships, water sports, sailing, ferries – children love being in, on and around water. Head for H_2O.

3   **Discover animal magic.** Children can't get enough of animals, so look out for urban farms, pet shows, safari parks, agricultural shows, nature trails, petting zoos and aquariums.

4   **Resolve the puzzles.** Get the old grey matter working overtime. Join in with a treasure hunt or get lost in a hedge-maze. Places such as Hampton Court and Chatsworth House are great places to start.

5   **Get messy.** Mud, mud, glorious mud. Depending on his age, your child will love getting down and dirty with quad bikes, paint-balling, pony-trekking, off-road driving and trail biking.

6   **Find out more about food.** Take your child to food fairs and festivals, cafés and restaurants, cooking

classes, fudge kitchens, farm shops and outdoor barbecues. All these will get your child fired up about where his food comes from.

7 **Here comes the science...** Explosions, crazy experiments and mad professors. Who said science had to be boring? Get hands-on at places such as the Science Museum in London or the Magna Adventure Centre in Sheffield.

8 **Go back to the Industrial Revolution.** Working textile mills, railway museums, trams, mining museums... children are fascinated by the noise, grime and grim stories that come with tales from our industrial heritage.

9 **Go for a ride.** Trains, planes, car and bikes – there are lots of museums and open days where children can climb on and enjoy the thrill of different types of transport.

10 **Do something completely different.** Visit a chocolate factory, watch the Red Arrows, go to the races, take in a show – it might involve a bit of extra planning, but your child will be talking about it for weeks!

Family support

Raising a family is the hardest thing you'll ever do. Most of us need outside support at one time or another, but it's not always easy to ask for help. Seeking help – whether it's financial, practical or emotional – can sometimes feel like an admission of failure. It's not. Parents and children who can admit to their difficulties are often the most resilient and able to deal with problems when they arise. Here are 10 organizations designed specifically to offer back-up and advice when you need it.

1   **Parentline Plus.** Parenting worries? Talk to Parentline Plus's free, confidential helpline on 0808 800 2222. This organization also offers advice via email and runs groups and workshops. Visit the website at www.parentlineplus.org.uk.

2   **ChildLine.** If your child has a problem she doesn't feel she can talk to you about, let her know she can always call ChildLine. Children and young people can phone free and confidentially on 0800 1111.

3   **Connexions Direct.** Older children between the ages of 13 and 19 might prefer to talk to someone at Connexions Direct (080 800 13 2 19). Advisers are trained to offer confidential advice and practical help about issues surrounding teenage life, including bullying, sexuality and drugs.

4   **Relate.** Being a parent can have a profound effect on your relationship. Relate offers advice, relationship counselling, sex therapy, workshops, mediation, consultations and support face-to-face, by phone and through its website (www.relate.org.uk).

5   **SureStart.** The government has designed the SureStart programme to help parents give their child the best

start in life. Its website (www.surestart.gov.uk) is a great source of information on finding and paying for early education and childcare.

6 **Gingerbread.** Lone parents can find specific help and advice through Gingerbread (www.gingerbread.org.uk). It also offers support via an expert and confidential free phone service on 0800 018 4318, and over 200 local self-help groups.

7 **Children's Legal Centre.** This is a charity concerned with law and policy affecting children. Its website (www.childrenslegalcentre.com) is a great source of information for children and parents on a wide variety of subjects, including contact, parental responsibility, residence and school attendance.

8 **Contact a Family.** A fantastic organization offering advice and support to parents of children with special needs and disabilities, including a website (www. cafamily.org.uk) and free helpline 0808 808 3555.

9 **Family Mediators Association.** During a divorce or separation, tempers can get frayed. Use a family mediator to help you and your partner resolve your disputes, reduce hostility and improve chances of long-term cooperation. Visit www.thefma.co.uk or call free on 0808 200 0033 for more information.

10 **Young Minds.** A charity committed to improving the mental health of all children and young people. Call 0800 018 2138 or visit the Parents' Information Service at www.youngminds.org.uk.

Financial aid

Never has the cost of bringing up children been so high. For many families it can be a real struggle to make ends meet. If you are expecting a child, raising your own, or looking after someone else's, you are almost certainly entitled to various kinds of financial aid, depending on your circumstances. Lone parents, carers of disabled children, and widows are also entitled to different kinds of help. Unfortunately, not all benefits come from the same organization, so it can be tricky knowing who to contact for what. Often if you are entitled to one kind of benefit, such as Income Support, it is recommended that you apply for others too. Here's a quick summary of the agencies that can help.

1   **Jobcentre Plus.** The Department for Work and Pensions (DWP) manages most benefits for families, such as Income Support, through Jobcentre Plus offices. Find your nearest office at www.jobcentreplus.gov.uk or look in Yellow Pages.

2   **Child Support Agency.** The Child Support Agency (CSA) is also part of the DWP and is responsible for assessing and collecting child maintenance from absent parents. Visit www.csa.gov.uk or call 08457 133133 for general queries on any aspect of child support.

3   **HM Revenue and Customs.** HMRC deals with Child Benefit, which every child gets, Guardian's Allowance, Child Tax Credits (to help with childcare costs) and Working Tax Credits (for working parents). Visit www. hmrc.gov.uk.

4   **Your local council.** Housing Benefit and Council Tax Benefit are handled by your local council on behalf of the DWP. It may also award educational bursaries, free school meals, school clothing grants and disabled student allowances.

5 **Healthy Start.** You may qualify for free milk, fresh fruit and vegetables, infant formula and vitamins under the Healthy Start scheme. Request a Healthy Start application form by calling 08701 555 455, or visit www.healthystart.nhs.uk.

6 **UCAS.** If your family is on a low income and your child is going to university, he may be entitled to financial help. Unlike student loans, these grants do not have to be repaid. Search for courses, fees, bursaries and financial support at the Universities and Colleges Admissions Service (www.ucas.co.uk).

7 **The Family Fund.** This is a government-funded charity covering the whole of the UK. Based on families' views and needs, it provides grants to those with severely disabled or seriously ill children. Visit www.familyfund. org.uk.

8 **Family Welfare Association.** This organization (www. fwa.org.uk) provides grants towards fuel bills, clothing and household expenses for people in need. It also has an advisory service offering guidance to students seeking secure funding for post-16 education and training.

9 **Children Out.** The Funds-4-Fun scheme run by this organization offers small grants to help provide new toys and special play equipment for disadvantaged and disabled children. It also provides fun days out, holidays and activities. Visit www.childrenout.org.uk.

10 **Family Holiday Association.** This charity can provide financial assistance towards holidays for families on low incomes. Visit www.fhaonline.org.uk.

First love

Most people experience first love during their teens. It's a particularly intense and overwhelming time, although most dating relationships at this age last for only a brief period. However, that doesn't mean first love is trivial. The experience of it helps teenagers learn about their own identity and feelings. It also teaches them the importance of intimacy and how to develop close relationships in the future. The big questions are, how, as a parent, do you handle your child's first relationship, and what do you do if you don't like her choice of partner?

1 **Try to remember what you felt like.** We all remember the power and intensity of our first love. Put yourself in your teenager's shoes – it may help you to get a bit of perspective.

2 **Steer clear of Romeo and Juliet.** Teens love the idea of forbidden love. There's nothing like disapproving parents to push two teens closer together. Try to be supportive.

3 **Don't panic.** Don't worry that your child has 'settled down' too soon if he or she has a girlfriend or boy-friend. Early relationships tend to burn out quickly – one survey showed that at 15, relationships last an average of only three or four months.

4 **Consider the phase your child is in.** There are three phases of love – initial lust, falling in love, and long-term attachment. Teens experience lust more readily, but often fail to enter the attachment phase. Chances are, the relationship is based on looks and won't last.

5 **Respect your child's feelings.** When teenagers fall in love, psychologists say that the experience mimics the strong bond between mother and infant. First love

is more intense than subsequent relationships, so don't poke fun or belittle your child's experience.

6 **Don't expect rationality.** Research has shown that when teenagers are in love it has a similar effect on their brains as using cocaine. No wonder they're behaving oddly!

7 **Understand lessons in love.** Don't discourage first love – it's a valuable life lesson. Young relationships encourage your child to be open, sharing and trusting, all of which help her develop the skill of intimacy.

8 **Talk about sex.** You may be struggling to come to terms with the idea of your child having a relationship, but she needs your support to help her handle her sexuality in a mature and safe way (see page 143).

9 **Don't believe the myths.** TV programmes and films may give parents the impression that teenagers are unstoppable bed-hoppers, but the truth is quite different. Most young people only have sex within a lasting relationship.

10 **Be encouraging when it all goes wrong.** Don't say 'I told you so', even if you didn't like your child's choice. Try to be there to listen. Encourage her to get out and meet new friends. And spoil her rotten – now's the time for treats, pampering and lots of attention.

Friendship

Have you noticed that some children seem to make friends easily, while others find the whole process a bit of a mystery? As a parent, it can be agony watching from the sidelines. Both parents and experts agree that social skills are just as important as academic performance, but they don't always come naturally. Here are 10 tips to help your child make friends.

1   **Accept that children vary.** Start with the premise that not everyone can be the life and soul of the party. Some children prefer only one or two close friends, while others surround themselves with a wider circle. It also doesn't follow that sociable parents will produce sociable children.

2   **Be a good listener.** Your child may want to voice his concerns about making friends or a friendship that seems to be going wrong. Provide a sympathetic ear without necessarily offering advice – he might just need to get things off his chest.

3   **Plan a solution.** If your child does want help, try to solve the problem together. Ask 'what ifs?' to help your child prepare what to say and do in different social scenarios.

4   **Notice problem behaviour.** Does your child have any habits that might be making friendships difficult? Is he very bossy or argumentative, for example? If so, gently point him towards alternative behaviour.

5   **Make an open house.** Create an environment that encourages your child to bring friends home. Invite pals around for play-dates or a meal. Friendships often flourish away from the competitive atmosphere of school.

6   **Join our club.** Does your child have specific interests or a hobby? Clubs are a great way for children to connect with like-minded individuals and really be themselves, away from parents and teachers.

7   **Encourage sharing.** Children who can share tend to make friends more easily. Sharing shows that you like, trust and value the other person, all of which are vital in growing friendships.

8   **Have a party.** Celebrations and group activities are a great way to forge new friendships and cement existing ones. Ask your child if he'd like you to organize a barbecue, birthday party or sleepover.

9   **Share the school run.** Not only is car-pooling a great way to save on petrol, but sharing the school run with other parents will provide a welcome opportunity for your child to mix with others.

10   **Talk to teachers.** Your child spends a large proportion of his day at school. As a result, teachers are often better judges of his social life than you are. Talk to them if you are worried about your child's friendships.

Getting involved

Parents often make the mistake of thinking that children want to be left alone. While we all need our own space, children included, getting involved is a vital part of parenting. Being interested and engaged in your child's life and interests makes her feel valued and important. It shows that you support her choices and trust her to make good decisions. Children with involved parents tend to do better at school, have higher self-esteem and better mental health. However, finding the right level of involvement isn't always easy.

1 **What does it mean?** Being involved is the same as being 'hands-on' – it means taking an active interest in your child's life, whether it's school, friendships, hobbies, opinions, interests, relationships or behaviour.

2 **Isn't that spying?** No. Children need privacy just as much as adults. Being involved means taking an interest without attempting to force your child to divulge everything. Being involved can also mean knowing when to give her space.

3 **How can I get involved?** Start talking. Let your child set the agenda – talk about how she feels about lessons at school, her friendship group, any good books she's been reading, what her favourite computer game is. Anything to get the ball rolling.

4 **Talk about your life.** You might have to get the conversation started with a gentle opener, such as 'I'm really enjoying my job at the moment – how's school for you?' or 'I saw a fantastic film the other day. Have you seen anything you liked recently?'

5 **Admit to problems.** Being open encourages openness in your child. Say 'I find it difficult to...' or 'Isn't it

annoying when...' and she may feel able to share her worries back.

6 **Make time.** Getting involved takes commitment – you need to have time for in-depth conversations and to take part in activities. Mark out time for your child and don't let anything get in the way. Use the 'Work/life balance' checklist on page 177 to help you.

7 **Get involved in school.** Your child spends a large part of her life at school, so use the 'Liaising with school' checklist on page 81 to get a better understanding of her schoolwork, interests and social life.

8 **Know the three Ws.** You can't choose who your child is friends with, but you can take an active interest in what she's doing. Always know *who* she is with, *where* she is and *when* she'll be back.

9 **Take family days out.** Spend time together as a family doing something you all enjoy. Feeling part of a functioning, happy family helps children deal with the insecurities of the outside world. Use the 'Family outings' checklist on page 57 for inspiration.

10 **Find a joint interest.** If possible, try to find an activity that you can enjoy together. Join a sports club, talk about films, share an interest in art or fashion, or find a board game or computer game you both like.

Grandparents

While grandparents can be an enormous source of support and advice for new parents, the relationship is also one that needs sensitive handling. Different parenting styles inevitably clash, and it can be tricky to cope with unsolicited advice, even if it is well meaning. On top of that, many families have two sets of grandparents, both of whom may be vying for time with your child. So how can you please everyone and still please yourself?

1 **Been there, done that, got the T-shirt.** Times have changed, but many of the rules of good parenting are still the same. If you think your parents did a good job raising you, why not ask them to pass on some of their skills and knowledge? They'll be thrilled to be asked.

2 **Learn how to be tactful.** There will be times when you disagree over the best way to bring up your child. Recognize that most advice from grandparents is given with good intentions – if you don't agree, tactfully let it go and have the courage to make your own decisions.

3 **Get professional back-up.** If grandparents are being particularly pushy with unwelcome opinions, you might want to arm yourself with expert advice from doctors, health workers or teachers. They'll have their fingers on current best practice.

4 **Don't expect childcare on tap.** Never take childcare for granted. Grandparents might seem like a great source of free childcare, but don't assume they'll always be pleased to step in. Book arrangements well in advance, and make sure it's OK for them to say 'No'.

5 **Offer something in return.** Childcare is demanding, and grandparents should feel that their contribution is valued. Is there something you could provide in return,

such as cooking a meal, help with shopping, DIY or a spot of gardening?

6 **Establish boundaries.** If grandparents are providing childcare, whether it's a few hours or a few weeks, be clear about how you would like your child to be cared for. You need to be confident that the grandparents will have the same views about mealtimes, safety, discipline, bedtimes and so on.

7 **Keep everyone in the loop.** It's unlikely that both sets of grandparents will spend equal time with their grandchild. Make a concerted effort to keep less involved grandparents in the loop – emails, phone calls, cards, letters, videos, visits, webcams – there are lots of ways to keep in touch.

8 **What's in a name?** Some grandparents feel too young to be called 'Grandpa' or 'Grandma'. While most of us get used to the names eventually, there's no reason your child can't call them by their first names or a made-up name, such as Oma or Pops.

9 **Be gracious about Granny.** You might have good reason to be annoyed with your parents or parents-in-law, but always try to talk about them in a respectful, loving way. Whatever your feelings, your child probably loves them to bits.

10 **Learn lessons for the future.** As a parent, the experience of juggling your child and his grandparents is an important one. When your child becomes a parent himself, try to remember the lessons you learnt and give him the space to make his own mistakes.

Hobbies

It's a wonderfully old-fashioned word, 'hobbies'. It conjures up images of small boys enthusing over steam engines or collecting stamps. For today's children, there are thousands of things to be passionate about, and it's great for them to have an interest. The whole point of hobbies is that they are practised for interest and enjoyment rather than grades or financial reward. And that's what makes them important – hobbies are about personal fulfilment rather than pleasing someone else. The fact that engaging in a hobby can lead to greater skills, knowledge and experience is just a welcome bonus.

1 **Give freedom of choice.** Let your child choose her own hobby. Hobbies are primarily about doing something purely for pleasure, so be sure to let your child choose her own. Suggest lots of different, unusual ideas if she's stuck for inspiration.

2 **Avoid taking over.** This is your child's hobby, not yours. It can be tempting to stand over her, giving helpful directions and hints, but that's a sure-fire way to zap the joy out of your child, not to mention the learning experience.

3 **Let your child be different.** Your child may have chosen a hobby that you don't see any value in, or you think is odd, but that doesn't mean it isn't very important to her. Never belittle your child's interests.

4 **Share your child's passions.** Talking about hobbies can be a real point of common ground between parent and child. Take an active interest in her pursuits and let her show you the results of her efforts.

5 **Be supportive.** Your child may need special equipment, clean sports kit, transport or adult supervision for her

hobby. Try to get the entire family to provide as much support as they can.

6 **Enjoy the therapeutic benefits.** Children who are struggling at school, lack confidence or have other problems may find a hobby a welcome distraction. Hobbies allow children to focus on something positive, with self-directed goals and creative outcomes.

7 **Remember that hobbies can become careers.** Lots of people, from amateur archaeologists to racehorse trainers, turn their hobbies into a career in later life. Explore the options when your child starts thinking about jobs and further education.

8 **Join a club.** Hobbies can be solitary activities, but it doesn't mean they can't be sociable. Encourage your child to join a club or society where she can meet like-minded friends.

9 **Make extra pocket money.** Some hobbies can help your child to earn extra pocket money, so don't discourage her entrepreneurial spirit if that's what she's keen to explore.

10 **Find yourself a hobby.** Set an example by throwing yourself into your own interests. Demonstrate that it's important to have time and space to pursue your own passions.

Holidays and travel

Not all holiday destinations are suitable for young families. And while some people are brave enough to backpack around the world with their toddler or teenager in tow, most parents just need a relaxing two weeks in a stress-free, safe environment. Child-friendly holidays are becoming much more popular, and the perfect way to meet other parents. They're also a great way to holiday with noisy young children without worrying about disapproving looks.

1   **Check out the internet.** There are some great websites that can help you. Among them is www.babygoes2.com, a totally independent website developed and run by parents. It's now considered to be one of the best information sources for anyone travelling with children.

2   **Forget noisy destinations.** You might still hanker after a clubbing until the early hours, but 'youth' resorts don't tend to make good family destinations. There is too much noise and booze, and not enough child facilities.

3   **Head for the water.** Children are happy to spend hours splashing about in a pool or at the beach, so try to head for somewhere with access to water and lots of shade.

4   **Self-cater.** Hotels can be a bit restricting for parents with young children. Self-catering holidays allow you to set your own routine, eat your own food and create a little home-from-home.

5   **Stay with friends.** If it's your first holiday away with your child, consider staying with some good friends. It'll give you a change of scenery without too much expense or forward planning.

6 **Start small.** If you're feeling nervous about travelling with a young child, do a 'dummy-run' holiday nearer to home. It'll be a great way to iron out any problems, without having to deal with language barriers or unfamiliar surroundings.

7 **Consider childcare.** Lots of travel companies now offer hotel packages that include access to reputable childcare or crèches, so you can enjoy the occasional evening out.

8 **BYO nanny.** Some parents take along their own nanny. This is a great option if you're already employing someone as a full-time childcarer because it rarely costs you any more than staying at home.

9 **Carry on camping.** If you were keen campers before the arrival of your offspring, there's no reason to stop now. Most campsites welcome families, and some even offer tents with separate bedrooms, kitchen equipment and child safety gates.

10 **Travelling with teens.** Look for a destination that will provide some adventure, activities and social events aimed at teens. Think about letting your child take a best friend for company.

Homework

No child likes getting homework, but it's an inevitable part of school life. The idea of after-school work is to extend the learning process into the home and teach children the skills of self-motivation and organized learning. It also helps them get through a larger curriculum than can be covered in the classroom alone. But doing homework is a learnt skill, like any other school subject, and one that takes practice and self-reliance. Here are 10 tips for helping your child get to grips with her workload.

1 **Don't do the homework yourself.** While you could probably get it done in half the time, and with fewer mistakes, your child needs to learn to do it herself. Her teacher will also have a pretty good idea if an adult has completed a project.

2 **Sort out a routine.** Homework is non-negotiable: it's a fact of school life. Arrange for it to be done as part of the after-school routine, with set time limits and breaks, and arrange a treat upon successful completion.

3 **Make it comfortable.** A quiet space with no distractions, a good table and comfortable chair, enough light, pens, paper, a ruler and other necessary equipment are always helpful.

4 **Coming unstuck?** If your child really cannot do or understand a particular piece of homework, arrange to see her teacher to discuss the problem as soon as possible. It's very easy for children to slip behind and lose confidence.

5 **Taking too long?** Perhaps the work is too hard and needs to be modified to suit your child's level of ability.

She may also be over-conscientious and could be doing too much. If reading takes a long time, check she isn't struggling with poor eyesight or dyslexia. Talk to the school.

6 **Give lots of praise.** Support your child's homework efforts. Give lots of praise and encouragement for getting down and completing the task. Take the trouble to read through something she would like you to see, and focus on the positives.

7 **Enable internet access.** Children often need a computer as a research tool and word processor. Be careful to stress, however, that downloading essays from the internet is the same as cheating. Teachers and examiners are wise to this, and students who cheat will be penalized.

8 **Don't stand over your child.** No one likes to be pushed or forced to act under pressure. Give your child space and trust her to get on with it by herself.

9 **Homework not being done?** If this is the case, sooner or later the school will call you in for a talk to try to resolve the situation. Work together to find a sensible solution.

10 **Encourage your child to check her own work.** Get your child into the habit of checking her own homework before handing it in. Teachers frequently downgrade fantastic pieces of work for silly mistakes and spelling errors. Neatness and good presentation also go down well.

Immunizations

There's no doubt about it – immunizations are the best way to protect your child from serious illness. Before the days of vaccines, young children regularly contracted life-threatening diseases, such as measles, whooping cough and polio. Nowadays we rarely see these diseases in the UK. The way immunizations work is wonderfully simple. Your child is given a very weak form of the disease, usually as an injection. This amount of a disease isn't enough to make your child poorly, but will stimulate his immune system to produce antibodies that will help him fight off any future infections.

Below you'll find the current NHS guidelines for your child's immunization 'timetable', but your GP or health visitor should remind you when the next one is due. Some vaccines have to be given only once, while others require a booster jab to keep up levels of protection.

1 **At two months old.** Your child should be immunized against diphtheria, tetanus, whooping cough, polio and haemophilus influenzae type B (Hib). The child vaccination schedule was changed in September 2006 to include a vaccine to protect against pneumococcal infection (which can cause meningitis) called Heptavalent Pneumococcal Conjugate Vaccine (PCV). As part of the changes, children under two who have missed the new scheduled vaccinations will be offered a single dose of PCV as part of a catch-up programme.

2 **At three months old.** Your child should be immunized against diphtheria, tetanus, whooping cough, polio and Hib again. He will also be given the meningitis C vaccine.

3 **At four months old.** Your child should be immunized against diphtheria, tetanus, whooping cough, polio, Hib, meningitis C and PCV again.

4 **At 12 months old.** Your child should be immunized against Hib and meningitis C again.

5 **At 13 months old.** Your child should be immunized against PCV again. He will also be given the measles, mumps and rubella (MMR) vaccine.

6 **At 3–5 years old.** Your child should be immunized against diphtheria, tetanus, whooping cough and polio again, as well as MMR.

7 **At 13–18 years old.** Your child should be immunized against diphtheria, tetanus and polio again. Instead of automatically being given the tuberculosis or TB vaccine at age 14, a new targeted programme was introduced in September 2005. Now only children who are considered at high risk of TB will be given the vaccine (including children living in areas with a high rate of TB, or whose parents or grandparents were born in a country where there is a high incidence of the disease).

8 **Possible extra vaccines.** Your child may need another tetanus immunization. This booster is required only for children whose vaccinations are *not* up to date and who are at risk of getting tetanus following injury.

9 **Holiday immunizations.** Vaccinations are also available to people travelling to areas where there may be serious diseases, such as malaria, typhoid or yellow fever. Ask your GP well before your trip for advice about which vaccines you and your child will need.

10 **Need more information?** For more information on all types of immunizations, visit NHS Direct (www.nhsdirect.nhs.uk), or talk to your family doctor.

Independence

One of the hardest things to give your child is independence. As loving parents, we want to protect our children from the outside world with all its disappointments and dangers. We also struggle with the idea of our children growing into adults and leaving the nest. It's both painful and wonderful watching your child gain skills and confidence that allow her to move on, but it's a vital part of parenting. Here are 10 tips that will encourage your child to become independent.

1   **Give children choices.** Learning to make decisions and take the consequences of your own choices is a huge part of growing up. Provide your child with opportunities to choose between things – just make sure you offer choices that both of you can live with.

2   **Don't jump in.** The process is often as important as the end result. Let your child attempt things by herself, and don't be too quick to jump in. Offer help but don't make it compulsory; your child will learn a lot by thinking through a complex problem or difficult scenario.

3   **Explore problems together.** If your child comes to you with a tricky question, don't rush to provide a complete answer. Try to work out the solution together; this will encourage your child to participate in the problem-solving process.

4   **Phone a friend.** Mum and Dad don't always have all the answers. Encourage your child to seek advice or information from lots of different sources, including friends, family, teachers, experts or your local library. Your child will love playing detective.

5   **Respect different opinions.** As your child becomes more independent, she will start to think for herself.

Respect the fact that she may have different opinions from you; you don't have to agree, but it doesn't mean you shouldn't listen.

6 **Allow young toddlers to choose.** Start encouraging independence from an early age. Toddlers really benefit from being given small choices to make – which story to read, what flavour yoghurt to eat and so on.

7 **Encourage independence for pre-schoolers.** Pre-schoolers are ready to take bigger steps towards independence. Encourage your little one to take part in daily activities, such as putting away her clothes, setting the table or helping to feed the pets.

8 **Help your child extend her independence.** Once children reach school age, their life will be full of choices. Encourage your child to make independent decisions about friends, school projects and hobbies.

9 **Give teens responsibilities.** Being given responsibility is a large part of developing independence in your teenager. Allow her to make financial decisions with her pocket money, for example, or encourage her to find part-time work.

10 **Provide a safety net.** Independence is best fostered in warm, loving families. That's because children feel secure and confident enough to strike out on their own. Always let your child know how much you love and value her.

Liaising with school

Your child will spend most of his formative years in the school environment. Parents can sometimes feel 'shut out' of their child's schooling, or bewildered by the decisions that schools take. Have your say. Get involved. Sit on a committee. On the whole, schools really welcome all the help and involvement they can get from parents. What's more, you'll be in a much better position to help your child make the most of his education.

1 **Make the most of parents' evenings.** These are a chance for you to meet your child's teachers first hand, and the perfect opportunity to discuss how well your child is doing academically and in school generally.

2 **Follow home/school agreements.** All schools now have agreements that set out what they are trying to achieve and the parents' role in it. Take it seriously: children achieve more when schools and parents work together.

3 **Join the Parent Teacher Association.** Most schools have a PTA that gets involved in all sorts of activities, such as fundraising and organizing events. If you want to become a member, contact the PTA at your child's school.

4 **Consider standing as a governor.** All schools have a governing body working with the head teacher and senior management to ensure pupils get the best education. If you want to get on the governing body, look out for the next election at your school or contact your local education office.

5 **Help on school trips.** Parents can offer to help out on school trips. Just remember that you're not going along responsibility-free; although you are not held as

accountable as teachers, you must accept the normal common law duty of care to act as a 'responsible parent' towards *all* the children.

6 **Liaise with the school nurse.** School nurses work with pupils, teachers and parents to promote well-being at school. If your child has any specific health problems, be sure to liaise with the school nurse. She'll need to know if your child has particular allergies and medical requirements.

7 **Could you give a talk?** If you've got an interesting job or hobby – zoo keeper, actor, cameraman – why not ask the school if you can give a talk to the children? This works particularly well with young children, before the 'embarrassment factor' kicks in.

8 **Help out.** Some schools like parents to help out, whether it's in the classroom or with after-school activities. Children can really benefit from the support offered by an extra pair of hands – just make sure your child is happy to have you along.

9 **Arrange a one-off meeting.** Your child's teacher or the school head should always be willing to set up a meeting about any specific worries you may have. Call the school secretary to arrange a time.

10 **Need to make an official complaint?** If you've had no luck resolving a problem through the school, contact your Local Education Authority. All LEAs are required to have a complaints procedure, and you need to put your point in writing.

Lone parenting

Raising children is hard enough when there are two of you, so it's doubly difficult when there's no one to share the ups and downs. The trick is to know *what* you're entitled to and *how* to ask for help when you need it. One Parent Families (www. oneparentfamilies.org.uk), a charity promoting lone parents' welfare, is an excellent source of advice and support. It offers the following survival tips for lone parents.

1 **Seek financial support.** Make sure you receive all the financial help you are entitled to. Splitting up from your partner might mean you become eligible for new benefits or Tax Credits, or are now entitled to a higher amount. Call the Lone Parent Helpline on 0800 018 5026 for information about what you are entitled to.

2 **Know your housing rights.** After a relationship breakdown and/or separation, you will usually have the right to remain in your home. Contact Shelterline for free housing advice on 0808 800 4444. You can also get advice from your local Citizen's Advice Bureau (www.citizensadvice.org.uk).

3 **Have you experienced violence or harassment?** Women can contact the 24-hour National Domestic Violence freephone helpline on 0808 2000 247 for advice or for somewhere safe to stay. Men who are experiencing violence should call Mankind on 0870 794 4124 for support and referral.

4 **Set up child maintenance.** Try to come to an agreement with your ex-partner. However, if this is not possible, contact the Child Support Agency national helpline on 08457 133 133. This organization can calculate and collect maintenance on your child's behalf.

5 **Tackle isolation and loneliness.** You might find that it helps to share experiences with people who have

been through the same thing. Contact Gingerbread on 0800 018 4318 for support groups in your area. For support and advice about parenting, contact Parentline Plus on 0808 800 2222.

6 **Help with childcare costs.** If you are working, you might get help towards childcare costs through Working Tax Credit – call the Tax Credits helpline on 0845 300 3900. If you are thinking of looking for work or training, you might get help with childcare costs through the New Deal for Lone Parents on 0800 868 868.

7 **Consider flexible working.** You have the right to ask your employer to consider a request for flexible working to change your hours and/or your patterns of work. You may also have the right to unpaid parental leave. For more information call the Lone Parent Helpline on 0800 018 5026.

8 **Get your Council Tax discount.** If you are the only adult in your household, you will qualify for a 25 per cent discount on your Council Tax. Students and older children for whom you still receive Child Benefit do not count as adults. Contact the Council Tax department at your local authority.

9 **Open your own bank account.** If you have a joint bank account and/or credit card with your ex-partner, contact the bank to cancel it and open your own bank account. You will need this for any Tax Credit and/or benefit payments you are entitled to, as benefits are no longer paid by order book.

10 **Make a will.** It's essential to make a will so that any property you own is distributed in the way you want, and your wishes about your child are considered. You might also need to alter any will you made before you separated from your ex-partner. For more information call the Lone Parent helpline on 0800 018 5026.

Mealtimes

Only 64 per cent of British teenagers regularly sit down to a meal with their parents. Compare that with Italy, where 93 per cent of teens take the time to dine with Mum and Dad, and you can see why some nutritionists claim that family meals are a thing of a past. The figures don't look much better for younger children either – just under half of all toddlers never sit down to eat with the whole family – but mealtimes *really* matter. Not only do they provide the family with an opportunity for conversations and laughter, they also lead to better nutrition because parents have greater control over the quality and quantity of the family's food choices. Getting your child to the table, however, is a different matter...

1 **Start early.** Even babies and toddlers thrive on sitting up at the table; it encourages them to eat properly, improves their speech and social skills, and tempts them to try new foods.

2 **Make mealtime a priority.** Emphasize the importance of eating meals together. Choose specific 'family meal-times' and write them on the calendar, even if it's just once or twice a week.

3 **Give choice over food.** If children take part in making a meal, they're more likely to eat it. Take your child food shopping and ask her to choose three fruits or three vegetables she'd like to eat during the week.

4 **Help your child to be a little chef.** Children get a real thrill from the whole family tucking into something they've prepared. CBeebies' *Big Cook Little Cook* is a fabulous place to start (www.bbc.co.uk/cbeebies/bigcooklittlecook).

5 **Create something for everyone.** If your child doesn't like cooking but wants to be creative, she can prepare

the meal in other ways, perhaps by choosing colourful table napkins or designing name tags.

6 **Make breakfast easier.** Are mornings a mad dash of washing, dressing and stuffing down a bowl of cereal? If you're struggling for time in the morning, try preparing your child's clothes and packed lunch the night before, and setting the alarm for 10 minutes earlier.

7 **Have fun with table talk.** Out of the habit of family conversations? The Back to the Table campaign, which promotes healthy eating and fun ways to get children to have a balanced diet, suggests trying FSGB (something Funny, something Sad, something Good, something Bad), where everyone tells a story from the day that fits into one of those categories. It's a good way to find out what went on in your child's day and to let her know about yours. Check out the Back to the Table website (www.raisingchildren.co.uk/btt_2005/home.asp) for more ideas.

8 **Eat out together.** Your child will love being given the opportunity to choose things from a menu, eat with different utensils and order from a waiter. Try as many different foods as possible.

9 **Teach good manners.** Teach your child to say 'please' and 'thank you' as soon as possible – good manners are a way of showing respect for others, and will help her feel more confident in social situations when she's away from home. It's also good practice to get all the family to thank the 'chef' at the end of a meal.

10 **Avoid a battleground.** Keep gripes and conflict away from the table. Postpone negative conversations about schoolwork or behaviour until another time.

Mobile phones

According to Ofcom, two-thirds of children aged 8–15 now own a mobile phone. As parents, we feel reassured that our children can call home in an emergency, and for children it offers much more – endless hours of interacting with friends, visiting websites, listening to music and taking photos. But with this new technology has come a new set of problems – text bullying, mugging, phone 'addiction', spiralling phone bills and potential health risks. So what's a responsible parent to do?

1   **Limit functionality.** It won't make you popular, but don't buy your child an all-singing, all-dancing phone. Just get him one that has the basic functions so that he can call or text friends and family. Young children might like a Teddyfone – it emits 10 times less radiation and is designed to deter muggers. Visit www.teddyfone.com.

2   **Be web wise.** Access to the internet brings with it problems of inappropriate downloads and expensive ringtones. It also exposes your child to online chatrooms. Don't get a WAP-enabled phone, or if you do, at least make sure your child is cyber-smart (see page 27).

3   **Talk to the operator.** If you want your child to have some web access, speak to the network operator about filtering certain sites and services from his phone.

4   **Get phone-savvy.** Don't let your child be a victim of phone scams. Tell him *never* to reply to unsolicited text or answerphone messages, and not to give his number out to strangers.

5   **Pay as he goes.** Children spend on average £10–£15 per month on their mobiles. Get your child a Pay As You Go phone so that you can keep an eye on his spending

and avoid spiralling bills. Make sure all the family is on the same network for free calls.

6 **Don't be a statistic.** Children are five times more likely to be mugged for their phone as adults. Tell your child to keep his phone out of sight when not in use, and security mark it with your address and postcode using a UV pen. If your child is mugged, tell him not to fight back.

7 **Take care with photos and videos.** Encourage your child to think carefully before he sends images of himself or friends to others. Once a digital image leaves his phone, it can end up anywhere.

8 **Know the health risks.** Children are three times more susceptible to radiation than adults. Current health advice is that children under the age of eight should not use mobiles *at all*, and those between eight and 16 should use them only in an emergency.

9 **Beware bullying.** One in five young people has been bullied via a mobile phone or the internet. If your child is being bullied, take it seriously and use the 'Bullying' checklist on page 15 to nip it in the bud.

10 **Avoid phone addiction.** Mobile phones can become more than a habit. Children have been known to rack up thousands in phone bills, or to become addicted to calling or texting. If you're worried about your child's phone behaviour, call Parentline Plus for helpful advice on 0808 800 2222.

Mood swings

When you think of mood swings you immediately think of teenagers. But children of all ages can experience sudden changes in temper, even toddlers. Parents are often left reeling, wondering where such violent outbursts or sullen sulks come from. But don't panic – mood swings are as much a part of childhood as grazed knees and bedtime stories.

1 **Identify the trigger.** Can you put your finger on what is setting off a mood swing? Is it when she is frustrated, lonely or bored, for example? Could you be doing something to ameliorate potential triggers, or intervene when you see a mood swing coming on?

2 **Make a note.** Try to chart your child's mood swings. Are they getting worse or starting to interfere with her school life or friendships? Is your child slipping into depression? Talk to your family GP if you think things are starting to get out of hand.

3 **Offer mood-boosting foods.** Mood swings can be a sign of a poor diet. Stable moods require stable insulin levels and blood sugar, so give your child foods that release energy slowly, such as porridge, oat cakes, brown rice, wholegrains and beans (see page 39).

4 **Promote the feel-good factor.** Mood swings can be a sign of low self-esteem. Help your child discover something that she loves doing – it'll give her confidence, and mood, a real boost (see page 29).

5 **Check your child's general health.** Lack of sleep and a sedentary lifestyle can also contribute to mood swings. Make sure your little one is getting enough shut-eye (see page 149) and keeping active (see page 55).

6 **Is everyone happy?** Children pick up on unhappiness around them. Is everything stable at home? Is your child exposed to endless family arguments or worries about money?

7 **Check the family history.** Moods can run in the family. If there's a history of mood problems, such as depression or anxiety, it might be worth checking things out with your GP.

8 **Be aware of hormones.** Don't forget the power of puberty. Fluctuating hormones are responsible for irritability, recklessness, aggression and depression in many older children (see page 119).

9 **Ease exam stress.** School life, especially as your child gets older, is dominated by peformance and assessments. Use the 'Exams' checklist on page 53 to help your child manage his stress levels.

10 **Keep going.** However bad it gets, just remember that family support and the loving bond you've already forged with your child will keep you all going through this challenging time.

Moving house

Moving house can be stressful for the whole family, especially children. They thrive on routine, so any changes to their surroundings can leave them feeling anxious and disorientated. The best way to limit the effects of a move is to be really organized and to communicate what's happening. Get your child involved in the planning and preparation – that way he'll know exactly what to expect during the coming weeks.

1 **Get talking.** Different ages of children need different involvement, but it's really important to keep talking, to include them as much as possible. Be honest; tell your child as early as you can why you're moving and what it will mean. Be positive and listen to his worries and his questions.

2 **Consider timing.** If you have a choice, think about fitting the move around your child's schooling. It may be easier for him to start the new school year when everyone else is settling into a new routine.

3 **Prepare for a new school.** Changing schools is stressful at the best of times. Visit the new school together, well ahead of the move, and get its help to prepare for the changes, including syllabuses, after school activities, uniform and kit requirements.

4 **Get your child involved.** Doing practical things for the move is a good way to involve your child in the whole process. He can choose his room, help plan changes and colours, do some packing of boxes, and make change-of-address cards.

5 **Make moving day run smoothly.** On the day of the move tell your child what's going to happen, and give

him some last-minute jobs to do. Some parents prefer to leave with the children, before the upset of the removal men dismantling the home. It's a long day for everybody. Have proper breaks and don't forget meals.

6 **Keep your child safe.** Moving is a prime time for accidents. Parents have their attention distracted, all the usual safety gates and locks are off, there are piles of boxes everywhere and people rushing around carrying stuff. If you can, have family or friends with you to take care of your child.

7 **Plan the journey.** If it's a long journey, plan it like a holiday trip. Take favourite toys and stories, and things to do. You'll know what will work best. Plan enough stops for food and toilets, and for time to stretch legs.

8 **Get off to a good start.** If you can get everyone warm and cosy, and produce some food and drinks, it's a good start. Familiarity helps too, so get your child's room organized first – it will give him a safe base to escape to and remake his own space.

9 **Help each other settle in.** All the family will need to work at this and support each other. The best way is to make time to talk together, and mealtimes can be good for this.

10 **Keep in touch.** Make the transition easier by encouraging your child to keep in touch with old friends, whether it's by email or phone. Make sure everyone, including schoolfriends, has your new contact details.

Music

Not only is music a great way for children to express themselves creatively, it also fires their imagination, releases emotions and lets them play with ideas. Children who regularly participate in music also have improved concentration, language development and social skills. Studies have even shown that experimenting with music increases a child's spatial awareness and mathematical ability. So what can you do to encourage your little one to love music?

1 **Start her early.** Babies and toddlers will love tapping out simple rhythms on upturned pots and pans. Play 'Copy Cat' with your child by clapping or tapping your feet to particular rhythms, or try making simple homemade instruments out of things around the house.

2 **Move to music.** Encourage your child to move to different types of music. Choose fast and slow rhythms. March, jump or crawl to the music. Reach up in the air to high notes and touch the ground to low ones.

3 **Play 'What's the Emotion?'** Ask your child to choose what emotion she thinks a piece of music has – is it sad or happy? Angry or excited? Can one piece of music have more than one feeling? How does a piece of music make her feel?

4 **Listen to different styles of music.** Expose your child to all sorts of music – jazz, pop, rock, reggae, blues, opera, funk, classical and folk. Even better, take her to live concerts, music fairs and local gigs.

5 **Make music.** If your child likes learning on the computer, consider a basic music software package – many allow you to play, record, manipulate and mix the music you make. Older children can learn the basics of DJ-ing and sound recording in their own bedrooms.

6 **Communicate your enthusiasm.** You don't have to play an instrument to be musical. Demonstrate your love of music by humming in the bath, dancing to your favourite track or singing along to the radio. Your child will soon see how much pleasure music can bring.

7 **Give access to music.** Buy second-hand instruments, hire them from school or your Local Education Authority, or rent one from a music shop. Encourage your child to borrow CDs from the local library, or to swap music with friends.

8 **Be a good audience.** Your child will get a lot of pleasure and pride from practising, rehearsing and playing to a crowd. It takes courage to play in public, so make sure there's lots of praise after a performance.

9 **Don't make practice a punishment.** Nothing will turn your child off music for life more effectively than if you make her practise as punishment. Don't push young children into long practice sessions – they won't be able to concentrate for very long periods.

10 **Talk about music.** Discuss music as a matter of course; it's a great topic for the dinner table. Talk about favourite artists, new bands, music styles, and likes and dislikes.

Nightmares

There are two types of distressing dream episodes – nightmares and night terrors. In a nightmare the person has disturbing emotions, usually fear and anxiety, and generally wakes up as a result. A night terror, on the other hand, seems to occur in a deeper sleep. Your child may thrash around, scream and can't be woken up or soothed. It can be scary to come face-to-face with a child in the middle of an episode, so here are some tips to help everyone get back to bed.

1 **Reassure your child that nightmares are normal.** Most children have nightmares. They appear to be a normal part of development and may reflect your child's struggle to deal with common childhood fears and problems.

2 **Get him talking.** Encourage your child to talk about his dreams. Could they be about anything he is anxious about at school or at home? Did he see something scary or violent on TV or hear a frightening story?

3 **Consult a professional.** Are your child's bad dreams getting more frequent or very frightening? It might be time to be referred to a therapist, who will let your child work through the nightmares by talking, drawing or painting the characters.

4 **Check medication.** Is your child taking any medicine? Certain prescription medications are thought to cause nightmares. Bad dreams can also be a symptom of withdrawal from a course of treatment. Talk to your GP.

5 **Consider the sleep routine.** Is your child getting enough sleep? Chronic tiredness and a disturbed bedtime routine can be a cause of bad dreams. Make sure he's getting enough shut-eye (see page 149).

6 **Avoid heavy meals.** Eating heavy meals shortly before bedtime may cause nightmares. Try getting your child to eat a light supper containing some sleep-inducing foods, such as dairy or soya products. Limit your child's caffeine intake.

7 **Is he too hot?** High temperatures or fevers can cause nightmares. Make sure your child's bedroom isn't too hot at night.

8 **Have comforting routines.** Develop a soothing bedtime routine so that your child feels relaxed when he falls asleep. A favourite blanket or soft toy can be comforting, as can a nightlight or keeping the door open.

9 **Start a dream journal.** Older children and teens might like to write down their nightmares. This 'dream journal' will help your child identify patterns and try to figure out how the nightmare relates to real life.

10 **Ease night terrors.** Night terrors are less well understood than nightmares, but seem to be more common in children than adults. Instead of trying to wake up your child, it's better just to make sure he is safe and help him return to sleep. If your child gets regular night terrors, try waking him before the usual time one occurs; this interrupts the sleep cycle and might prevent a night terror happening.

Obesity

Current estimates suggest that a quarter of all boys and a third of girls in the UK are classed as overweight or obese. Rather than just dismissing it as 'puppy fat', parents need to take the problem seriously as obesity is linked to all manner of health problems. Health experts are particularly worried about the link between childhood obesity and heart disease, certain cancers, high blood pressure, joint problems, emotional problems and type 2 diabetes. So what should you do if you think your child is overweight?

1 **Get your facts straight.** While you may suspect that your child is overweight it's important to get this confirmed by your GP. The usual test for adults, the Body Mass Index (BMI), is not a suitable measure for a growing child.

2 **Avoid fad diets.** Never put your child on a weight-loss plan designed for adults. Children need a healthy diet, not a low-carb, high-protein, high-fat or cabbage soup regime. Your GP will be able to give your child a healthy eating plan to follow.

3 **Get moving.** It's a simple equation – your child is not using up the calories she's ingesting. Rather than just focusing on food, encourage being active and taking part in exercise – this is a more fun way of losing the pounds (see pages 55 and 157).

4 **Make it a family affair.** Your child will feel singled out if she's the only one on a healthy eating plan. The solution is to get the whole family involved, and keep tabs on everyone's portions and food choices. That means mums and dads too.

5 **Keep the dairy.** A study in Denmark showed that dairy calcium stops fat being absorbed by the digestive

system, so include lots of low-fat dairy products, such as low-fat cheese, yoghurt and milk, in your child's diet.

6 **Have portions, not piles.** If serving bowls are left on the table, people will go back for seconds, regardless of whether they are hungry. Serve out portions on plates, and don't be too hasty to clear them away; evidence of how much you've eaten deters you from eating more.

7 **Get your child cooking.** The best way to get your child eating sensibly is to get her involved in choosing and preparing healthy meals – that way she'll see how much fat, sugar or salt *really* goes into every meal.

8 **Go low.** Swap high-fat, high-sugar and high-salt items for versions with reduced amounts – your child won't even notice the difference. Just watch out for artificial sweeteners or fat substitutes, which are often put in to boost the flavour.

9 **Turn off the TV.** Eating in front of the TV tends to lead to overeating. This is because we are distracted from the sensation of feeling full. Switch off the box and eat at the table.

10 **Breakfast like a king.** Studies have shown that children who eat breakfast consume less fat during the rest of the day than their counterparts who skipped this first meal. Breakfasters are also up to five times more likely to consume at least two-thirds of their recommended daily amounts (RDAs) of calcium, magnesium, riboflavin, folacin, phosphorus, iron and vitamins A, B_6 and D.

Opinions

There will come a time when your child's opinions differ from yours. At first, there might be differences over bedtimes or food choices, but as your child grows, it will soon become apparent that he's forming his own thoughts about lots of aspects of life, such as religion, politics and relationships. While it can be difficult to accept that our children are not carbon copies of ourselves, we should nonetheless encourage them to think through problems, formulate ideas and critically discuss them. Far from causing arguments and conflict within the family, allowing children independent thought is shown to produce more tolerant, socially confident and adaptable adults.

1 **Make the most of media.** Encourage your child to read or watch a wide variety of quality media, such as newspapers, magazines, news programmes and documentaries. Just make sure they're appropriate for your child's age.

2 **Discuss events.** Talk about what's happening in the world, from celebrity gossip to climate change. Encourage your child to think about the pros and cons of a situation, or what he would do if he was in charge.

3 **Make nothing off-limits.** Religion and politics used to be conversational no-nos. Research has shown that children who engage in collective critical discussions about moral, religious and philosophical issues are less likely to have racist, sexist or extremist opinions.

4 **Problem-solve.** Work problems out together because collaboration is the key to learning. What's important is the exchange of opinions and the ability to tap into another person's world.

5 **Be curious.** The best type of learning is driven by curiosity. Encourage your child to ask questions and

challenge commonly held beliefs. Explore new concepts and cutting edge ideas.

6 **Develop reasons.** Teach your child to justify his opinions. Many opinions fall by the wayside when challenged. Teach your child to express himself confidently and defend his ideas.

7 **Stamp out prejudice.** Children can pick up or hear racist/sexist opinions from friends and family members. Make it clear to your child that you find such opinions unacceptable and ignorant. Explain why these comments are harmful.

8 **Know the difference.** There's a big difference between having opinions and being opinionated. The best opinions are those based on experience and reflection rather than those that are stubbornly retained despite evidence to the contrary.

9 **Listen up.** Hearing other people's views is a big part of forming opinions. Encourage your child to respect other people's views, even if he doesn't agree with them.

10 **Don't panic.** It's not the end of the world if your child has an opinion that you think isn't very helpful. Views such as 'I'm never having children' or 'I want to leave school as soon as possible' often change as your child matures.

Out-of-school childcare and holiday schemes

Parents have a number of childcare options to cover the times when working hours extend beyond school hours.

The first is an Extended School. One in 10 schools currently opens between 8 a.m. and 6 p.m. to offer childcare and activities for children. Half of all primary schools and a third of all secondary schools are due to have extended opening hours by 2008. Out-of-school clubs or children's clubs also open before and after school, and during school holidays, to provide under-15s with safe and enjoyable places to play and do homework. Finally, Holiday Play Schemes are run by voluntary organizations and local authorities to give children places to play, meet friends and take part in a wide range of activities, such as sports or drama, arts and crafts or music.

The charity 4Children has over 20 years' experience as the leading national organization for out-of-school childcare. Its website (www.4children.org.uk) offers the following advice for parents looking for good-quality schemes.

1   **Is it registered?** Check if the club has been inspected and registered with Ofsted. For more information call 08456 404040, or visit www.ofsted.gov.uk, where you can search by postcode.

2   **Know who's in charge.** What qualifications and experience do the staff have?

3   **Check the child-to-carer ratio.** A minimum of one play worker per eight children is recommended.

4   **Is it striving to do better?** Find out whether the club is taking part in the Aiming High Quality Assurance scheme organized by 4Children.

5 **Be aware of the collection times.** What happens if you're late?

6 **What are the rules?** Different clubs have different rules. Find out what their approach is to discipline and how they manage children.

7 **Will you be kept informed?** Ask how the club goes about giving feedback to parents.

8 **How are decisions made?** Are parents involved in the decision-making process?

9 **Find out more.** For more information on finding out-of-school childcare, or setting up your own, visit www.4children.org.uk.

10 **Get help with costs.** Many families will be able to get help with childcare costs via Child Tax Credits. Visit www.hmrc.gov.uk or call 0845 300 3900 to see if you're eligible.

Parties

It seems that jelly and ice cream just don't cut it these days. Children's parties have become big business, with parents spending hundreds of pounds on professional entertainers, party planners and mass catering. There's no doubt that celebrations mean a lot to children. As they grow up, their birthdays take on more significance, and this, combined with their desire to impress friends, means that parties can become the most exciting events in their social calendar. But throwing money at a party isn't necessarily a guarantee of a brilliant bash. Much better to put a little love and effort into planning, preparation and party games.

1 **Plan ahead.** Get your child excited about the planning by encouraging her to draw up a guest list and write the invites. She'll also get a kick out of making up party bags, blowing up balloons and organizing games.

2 **Be selective.** There's a good reason why the tradition is to invite the same number of children as your child's age. Keep the numbers manageable or you'll be tearing your hair out. If your child doesn't like the idea of narrowing her guest list, explain that it will allow you to spend more per person or on a special activity.

3 **Have a back-up plan.** Always have a plan B. Outbreaks of illness amongst the guests or a spell of bad weather can soon put a dampener on the day – keep cheerful and do something even more fun to save the day.

4 **Keep it short but sweet.** Toddlers and pre-schoolers will struggle with any party longer than an hour. Older children can manage more, but how good is your staying power? Two or three hours is plenty.

5 **Pick a theme.** Let your imagination run wild. Theme the party around pirates, dinosaurs, animals, ghosts, fairies or aliens. Does your child have a favourite character or cartoon?

6 **Wear them out.** Party games, five-a-side football, water slides, karaoke, treasure hunts, bouncy castles, races, go-karts – plan plenty of activities to keep them busy.

7 **Make everyone a winner.** If you're going to play party games, remember that young children love to win. Make sure every guest wins at least one game or prize so that no one feels left out.

8 **Try a sleepover.** Sleepovers are great only for children who feel comfortable away from home. Stick to children over the age of 10, and check with parents that they'll make it through the night without tears.

9 **Don't try this at home.** Save your furniture from sticky fingers and host the party away from home. Ice rinks, water parks, swimming pools, sports centres, family restaurants and entertainment complexes all welcome groups of children.

10 **Should you have goody bags?** This is a tricky question. Goody bags can be an expensive business, and they aren't really needed if you make sure that every child has won a prize during the party. Why not help your child to write thank-you notes for all her guests a few days later instead?

Part-time jobs and pocket money

Money management is a key life skill. Most people only start thinking about finances when they're well into adulthood, but teaching children how to manage their money will make a marked difference to the rest of their life. For young children, pocket money is a chance to behave independently and make choices. Later on, when pocket money can't fund all your child's interests, a part-time job will help him to understand the complex relationship between different types of employment and financial freedom.

1 **Decide how much.** It's ultimately dependent on your financial situation, but (according to the 2006 Halifax pocket money survey) the average weekly pocket money in the UK is £6.30 for 7–12-year-olds and £9.76 for 12–16-year-olds.

2 **State what it covers.** Make it clear what this amount is expected to cover. Does it include money for other people's Christmas and birthday presents? Will it cover magazine subscriptions, snacks, cosmetics, or mobile phone bills?

3 **Encourage mini money experts.** Some children are natural spenders, while others are savers. This doesn't mean you can't encourage them to think about budgeting; even a six-year-old will understand the simple concept of putting away £1 a week towards something special.

4 **Try before he buys.** Every penny counts when it comes to pocket money. Get your child to try goods before he buys them. If he wants a CD, a computer game or a film, encourage him to borrow it from a friend or the library/video shop first. He might find he doesn't want it as much as he thought.

5 **Bank it.** Contrary to what you might think, most children like saving. Help them to open a bank or building society account. There are lots of special children's accounts with favourable interest rates, so shop around.

6 **Read all about it.** Children can make canny investors, especially when they learn what their money can earn. Offer them two interesting US guides – *Growing Money: A Complete Investing Guide for Children* by Debbie Honig and Gail Karlitz, and *Teenage Investor* by Timothy Olsen.

7 **Establish the ground rules.** While grandparents, aunties and uncles can all be generous sources of extra pocket money, just make sure they know the ground rules about maximum amounts and what the money can be spent on.

8 **Pay for home help.** Prepare a list of extra chores on top of the regular unpaid chores your child does so that she can earn extra money. Jobs could include gardening, cleaning and polishing the car, or ironing.

9 **Find additional income.** Between a quarter and a half of all teens have a part-time job. The most popular are a paper round and working in a shop. All these jobs can have unsociable hours, so make sure they don't interfere with schoolwork.

10 **Know the law.** There are strict rules relating to child employment, including 'No child may be employed under the age of 13' and 'No child may work before 7 a.m. or after 7 p.m. on any day, including school holidays'. Find out more at www.childrenslawcentre.org.

Peer pressure

The average secondary school child spends twice as much time with her friends as her family. It's no surprise, then, that when things go wrong parents are quick to blame bad behaviour on peer pressure.

While it's certainly true that children who socialize with friends involved in anti-social behaviour are more likely to get into trouble, parents often fail to realize that their children have sought these friendships in the first place. This is called 'peer preference' and it's a crucial factor in understanding why children choose certain friends. Research also shows that children who receive little support at home are the most likely to be influenced by their peer group.

1   **Avoid ultimatums.** Children don't respond to ultimatums. It's difficult to control who your child spends time with, and banning her from certain friendships may only result in making them seem more attractive.

2   **Recognize personal choice.** Children must make up their own minds. You can't choose your child's friends, but you can affect how easily she is led by others. Use the 'Confidence and self-esteem' and 'Opinions' checklists on pages 29 and 99 to help your child learn to formulate her own ideas.

3   **Lay strong foundations.** Older children often feel pressured into doing things that they're not ready to, such as having sex. Strong support from family and friends, combined with back-up from school, can help your child put this pressure in perspective.

4   **Encourage best friends.** As well as family being a major source of support against peer pressure, a good

friend is also crucial. A best friend can help your child to stand up against a larger peer group.

5 **Keep talking.** Contrary to what you might believe, research shows that many young people want to hear about things such as sex, relationships, and drugs from their parents, rather than getting a partial account from friends or the media. Keep the lines of communication open.

6 **Draw on older siblings.** If you think it might help, encourage your child to confide in an older sibling or cousin, especially one who might be able to relate to similar experiences and offer helpful advice.

7 **Develop outside interests.** If school is your child's only source of friendships, this can make it difficult for her not to conform. Encourage your child to balance things out with non-school interests and friendships.

8 **Don't sweat the small stuff.** Minor changes, such as a haircut or wearing black every day, are passing phases. Accept them as part of your child growing up, or you may face an even bigger battle on your hands.

9 **Tackle the big stuff.** If you think your child might be getting into serious trouble, a phone call to Parentline Plus on 0808 800 2222 will help you to work out your options without blowing your top.

10 **Don't worry too much.** Most children know right from wrong and grow into responsible, caring adults. Children tend to return to the ideas, values and beliefs gained from their parents – trust your child to make good decisions.

Periods

When a girl gets her first period it can be received with mixed emotions. While it can be exciting for her to think that her body is changing and growing up, it can also be frightening to think that her childhood is slowly coming to an end. Even though periods are perfectly normal, young girls can also feel squeamish or embarrassed by them. You can do a lot to reassure your child, however, and help with some of the practical and emotional problems that surround periods.

1 **Know when to expect them.** Girls start their periods at very different ages – as young as eight and as late as 17 – so offer reassurance about the wide variation. Other signs of puberty, such as developing breasts, indicate that they're about to start.

2 **Check your family history.** For mums, the age you started your period will be a clue to when your daughter might start hers.

3 **Explain everything.** While school lessons will certainly cover periods, girls often prefer hearing about them from Mum. Don't just focus on the bad stuff, such as the pain; celebrate the sense of maturity that having periods can bring.

4 **Get a good book.** If your daughter feels a bit embarrassed about talking to you, get her *The Period Book: Everything You Don't Want to Ask (But Need to Know)* by Karen and Jennifer Gravelle. It's funny, frank and highly recommended.

5 **Be prepared.** Your daughter won't want to be caught unprepared for her first period, so encourage her to carry a sanitary towel with her, or to keep one in her locker. If she forgets, tell her to ask a teacher or the school nurse.

6 **Pay for sanitary protection.** Tampons and towels are expensive – your daughter will struggle to pay for them herself. Ask her discreetly what she'd like you to get from the supermarket and leave them in an agreed place at home.

7 **Keep a diary.** Most girls' periods are irregular at first and won't happen every 28 days. Suggest to your daughter that she note down her 'on-days' in a diary so that she can start to see things settling down.

8 **Reduce period pain.** Encourage your child to use a hot-water bottle, have a warm bath or try mild painkillers. Exercise also works wonders, but if it gets really bad, talk to your GP about stronger pain relief.

9 **Encourage choice.** Most girls start with towels, but soon try tampons. Encourage your daughter to read the manufacturers' instructions and to use whatever feels most comfortable.

10 **Take advice for late starters.** Girls who exercise heavily, are very overweight or underweight, or have been suffering from illness or stress may find they start their periods late. If your daughter still hasn't started by age 16, it's time to talk to her GP.

Personal hygiene

Smelly socks. Stinky bedrooms. Sweaty armpits. Teenage hygiene is the butt of many jokes, but it's not so funny when you're on the receiving end. Children are notoriously sensitive about their personal hygiene, so it's important for parents to handle it with care. A few tweaks and top tips and your child will soon come up smelling of roses.

1 **Start young.** Young children rely on their parents to keep them clean. This is the perfect time to explain to your child that washing is an important part of keeping healthy and helping him to feel good about himself.

2 **Let shoes breathe.** The largest collection of sweat glands are in the feet. If your child has one pair of shoes for school, ask him to remove them as soon as he gets home so that they can dry out overnight. Even better, alternate between two pairs. Leather is better than plastic.

3 **Keep feet clean.** Your child needs to wash his feet at least once a day and dry them carefully. Pay attention to between the toes, where bacteria are prone to collect.

4 **Consider an anti-perspirant.** Fresh sweat is odourless, so your child shouldn't need to use a deodorant if he's washing regularly. If he sweats excessively, buy an unperfumed, paraben-free and aluminium-free anti-perspirant.

5 **Stay fresh.** BO is caused by stale sweat reacting with bacteria on the skin. Your teen needs to shower every day, taking care to wash his armpits, face, feet and between his legs with soap.

6 **Prepare for periods.** Your teen will sweat more when having a period, and will need to wash more often.

Menstrual blood also tends to smell when it reacts with air and warmth, so encourage your daughter to change sanitary protection regularly.

7 **Avoid bad breath.** Poor dental hygiene is usually the culprit behind bad breath, although smoking and strong foods, such as garlic and onions, can add to the problem. Ensure your child knows how to brush properly and visits the dentist regularly.

8 **Help your child have flowing locks.** Greasy hair is caused by the over-production of oil from the sebaceous glands beneath the skin. Your child should use a specially formulated shampoo and stick to oil-free conditioners. The use of hairdryers and straighteners should also be limited because heat stimulates oil production.

9 **Make a daily change.** Your teen should change his underwear and socks every day, and after sport. Cotton and wool clothes also wash more effectively than man-made fibres.

10 **Is there a deeper problem?** Caring about the way we look is important to our self-esteem. Is something making your child stop caring about his appearance? Is he depressed or being bullied?

Pets

Looking after a living creature is a great way of encouraging your child to develop an empathetic and caring attitude towards animals; it's wonderful for her to see the results of her efforts, whether it's a contented purr or the happy wag of a tail. New research has also shown more unexpected benefits of animal ownership; children with pets seem to have more stable immune systems, are less stressed and are less likely to suffer from depression. But not all animals make good family pets, and not all families are ready for the responsibility.

1 **Choose carefully.** Think about your lifestyle: is the family out all day? Does anyone in the family have allergies? Is the area safe for pets? Have you got the time for walks or grooming? Can you afford the food costs and vet's bills?

2 **Know your dogs.** Choose a breed that's calm and patient, such as a Labrador or golden retriever. Even better, get your dog neutered to make it less aggressive. Avoid small dogs – they're often highly strung and not able to tolerate boisterous children.

3 **Make friends with a cat.** Cats make friendly, independent family pets, but be sure to choose one that has a good temperament and likes to be petted. Ill or stray cats can behave unpredictably, so steer clear.

4 **Be careful of small animals.** Contrary to popular belief, small animals don't make good pets for young children. Hamsters, mice, rabbits and guinea pigs are all easily damaged if dropped or squeezed, so make sure your child is mature enough to handle them carefully.

5 **Relax with fish.** Fish can be relaxing, enjoyable pets for a child who's happy simply observing an animal's

behaviour without necessarily wanting to touch it. Place the fish tank where your child can't climb up, fall in, or pull the tank over.

6 **Avoid reptiles.** The life-threatening salmonella bacteria can be passed from turtles and terrapins, while snakes and lizards need adult care and attention to thrive. Avoid reptiles as family pets.

7 **Enjoy wild friends.** Don't want a pet? You can still get your child mad about animals. Encourage wildlife into your garden with a bird feeder, a bug box or a bee house. Make a container pond or worm farm. See www. bbc.co.uk/nature/animals/wildbritain for more ideas.

8 **Ensure adult supervision.** Always supervise children around dogs and other animals. Very little children are too young to understand the nuances of their pet's behaviour – it's your responsibility to keep both child and animal protected.

9 **Consider an old-timer.** If you're planning on getting a family pet, think about adopting an older cat or dog. Older animals tend to have more tolerant personalities and you also avoid the chaotic and messy house-breaking stage of kittens and puppies.

10 **If a pet dies.** Children can become very attached to family pets. A recent survey found that pets are included in many children's top five relationships – above a substantial number of human relationships. Allow your child to grieve.

Play

Much of today's parenting focuses on getting your child to behave, achieve and comply. While grades and good behaviour are important, we could be in danger of losing a vital part of childhood – the importance of play.

Play comes in many forms: 'rough and tumble' play is key to physical development and confidence; role-play enables your child to learn social skills and communication; and creative play is central to helping your child learn how to express himself and solve problems. Above all, play is your child's most natural and enjoyable way to learn.

1 **Find a safe place.** Children must have access to space and freedom to get the most from their play. This means that you need to direct your child towards safe, secure play spaces both indoors and outdoors (see page 129).

2 **Provide the right toys.** Parents often buy toys that can do a lot, instead of getting toys a child can do a lot with. The best toys need imaginative input from your child, so make sure you provide things such as crayons, building bricks, teasets and dressing-up outfits.

3 **Don't overdo the toys.** Too many toys can do more harm than good. Children become easily overwhelmed by the choices and can't concentrate on any one toy long enough to learn from it.

4 **Make time.** Make an effort to spend a fixed amount of quality playtime each day with your child. Not only will it make him feel valued and loved, it will also be a great stress reliever for you.

5 **Get down to their level.** Children love it when you join in. Just remember to keep things at your child's

level – making a game too complicated or competitive will only turn him off and undermine his confidence.

6 **Let your child direct play.** A large part of your child's life is controlled by you, so it's important to let him have some self-directed play. Choosing how and what to play encourages independence and experimentation.

7 **Engage in different types of play.** Children also need the opportunity to explore different kinds of play. Your child should experience playing by himself, alongside other children, in partnerships and in groups.

8 **Be the best toy in the world.** Larking about with Mum or Dad is worth more than the best-stocked toy cupboard. Pull faces, sing songs, make up silly rhymes and noises, pretend to be different animals, dress up as characters – your child will love it.

9 **Communicate through play.** If your little one is struggling with difficult emotions or feelings, consider play therapy. Conventional talking therapies are often inappropriate for young children, who struggle to put their feelings into words. Play therapy will allow your child to explore his feelings and to make sense of his experiences in a safe way.

10 **Make space for teen playtime.** Whatever your age, you need at least one thing in your life that you do for the sheer pleasure of it. Hobbies, sports, socializing – these are all just grown-up ways of playing.

Privacy

Why is privacy important? Most of our waking life is spent with other people. While it's important to socialize and interact, relating to other human beings involves constant compromise. Being alone, or anonymous, is very freeing because it allows us to be truly ourselves. As your child grows and becomes more independent, she will need more privacy. Growing up is tough enough without having to share every moment with the rest of the family.

1 **Establish bedroom boundaries.** Your child needs to have a space she can retreat to. Respect her privacy by always knocking and waiting before entering her room. Make sure other family members do the same (see page 7).

2 **Never read a diary.** It can be tempting to have a quick flick through. Be warned – get caught out and you'll lose your child's trust forever. If you're worried about something, talk to her directly.

3 **Talk about secrets.** There are good and bad secrets. Make sure your child knows the difference (see page 139).

4 **Expect physical privacy.** Children have the right to physical privacy – they need to know that their bodies belong to them alone. Expect your child to become more self-conscious about being naked as she gets older – this is normal and healthy.

5 **Allow time to talk.** It can sometimes take children a while to work out how to talk to you about a problem. Try not to pressure your child into talking if she's not ready – she'll come to you in her own time.

6 **Ban babyblogs.** Never post pictures of your child online – it's too difficult to control what happens to them. Consider a different way of sharing photos with far-flung friends and family.

7 **Ensure web privacy.** Your child shouldn't give out personal information to people he meets on the internet. See 'Computers and the internet' on page 27 for how to protect your child's online privacy.

8 **Know the Data Protection Act.** Any organization that collects personal information about people cannot pass it on to others without the individual's consent. (In the case of a child, parental consent would be required.) If you think a company has breached this rule, contact the Information Commissioner's Office via www.ico.gov.uk or call 08456 306060.

9 **Understand medical privacy.** What if your child goes to the doctor and doesn't want you to know? If your child is considered mature enough to understand the proposed treatment, the doctor must respect your child's wishes with regard to privacy and confidentiality.

10 **Take action in crisis situations.** Children need to know that you respect their privacy and that you won't act without their agreement. However, if you think your child is in a position of danger – perhaps considering suicide or criminal activity – you might have to breach her trust to do the right thing.

Puberty

Thank goodness times have changed. It's not that long ago that puberty was discussed only in hushed tones, and parents left children to struggle through it alone. Sex education in schools is much improved, and parenting styles have become more relaxed and open, making it easier for children to discuss their worries. It's still a tough time – what with all those hormones raging and hairs sprouting – but there are plenty of ways you can ease your child's transition into adolescence.

1 **Start early.** When your child hits eight years old, it's time to get talking. It might seem early to be discussing puberty, but remember that it's not uncommon for girls to start their periods at this age.

2 **Talk about differences.** Reassure your child that puberty happens at different ages and in different ways to every child. Everyone catches up eventually.

3 **Avoid the 'Big Talk'.** You can't cover everything in one marathon conversation. Keep an ongoing dialogue and if he doesn't ask, gently initiate conversations.

4 **Be honest.** Children are great at asking awkward questions, but it's important to be truthful. Assure your child that you will answer his questions honestly, and be sure to keep your promise.

5 **Get the tone right.** Not all the conversations have to be heavy going. Your child might prefer a lighter tone, or to have a giggle about things. Take your cue from him.

6 **Know your onions.** Are you ready and well informed if your child strikes up a conversation? Is it time to swot up on your biology basics? Try BBC Science's Human Body and Mind webpages (www.bbc.co.uk/sn).

7 **Talk to the school.** Get an idea of how much your child has already learnt in sex education classes. A discreet call to the school will soon get you up to speed.

8 **Buy the book.** Your child might prefer to read up first and then talk things over with you. *What's Happening to Me?* by Susan Meredith and Nancy Leschnikoff is a witty and sensitive starter for under-10s.

9 **Offer practical support.** Your child may need a raft of new things to get through puberty – offer to help your child stock up on essentials, whether it's a first bra, razor or tampons.

10 **Keep an eye on food and fitness.** Your child may feel as if his body is out of control. Encourage him to eat healthily and exercise to boost his self-image. Keep an eye out for crash diets and eating disorders, which commonly start at puberty (see page 49).——

Reading

Reading is a key skill. Not only is it vital for academic achievement and everyday life, but it's also a wonderful way to expand your child's imagination, help her relax and give her new and exciting experiences. Numerous studies have shown that the sooner you start sharing books with your child, the quicker she'll learn to read and the better she'll do at school. So what are you waiting for? Here are 10 top ways to help your child become bonkers about books.

1 **Make space for bedtime stories.** Reading aloud to your child will increase her desire to read independently. Studies show that regular bedtime stories also help children to improve comprehension and pick up vocabulary much more quickly. Set aside a regular story time every day.

2 **Have loads to read.** Surround your child with reading material. From comics to classics, children who are exposed to a wide variety of reading matter at home tend to do better at school reading tests.

3 **Enjoy family time.** There's nothing cosier than everyone in the family sitting in front of the fire and reading together silently. Can you set aside a 'family reading time' once or twice a week?

4 **Notice the words around you.** Encourage your child to read the words she sees in everyday life. Point out road signs, advertising boards, shop names, product descriptions and menus, for example.

5 **Love your library.** Libraries offer an endless supply of free books and other reading materials, as well as an enjoyable environment where your child can pore over books in peace. Younger children may also love any organized story sessions at the library.

6 **Liaise with school.** How quickly children pick up reading isn't necessarily an indicator of how bright they are. Be knowledgeable about your child's progress and find out how the teacher feels she is doing. Is there anything you could do to help at home?

7 **Keep an eye out for problems.** Issues that affect reading, such as dyslexia, poor eyesight or hearing, and Attention Deficit Disorder, are not always picked up until your child has fallen behind (see page 153).

8 **Get help promptly.** If you're really worried about your child's reading, talk to her teacher. If you are not satisfied with the response given, approach the head teacher. Failing that, a complaint to the school's governing body or the Local Education Authority tends to get things moving.

9 **Think beyond books.** You can use a whole host of reading aids to help your child progress. Computer games, audio books, magazines, DVDs and educational TV programmes all have their part to play in making reading fun.

10 **Show your enthusiasm.** Even if you're not a particularly strong reader, your child will love seeing you enjoying books; never give the impression that reading or bedtime stories are a chore. Your reaction to her reading is also vital – be sure to heap on praise for her efforts.

Respect

Newspapers often claim that today's children have 'no respect'. But what do they mean? The term is often used as shorthand to describe a group of behaviours that seem to annoy adults – talking back, swearing, damaging property and being cheeky. But it's more subtle than that; respect is about understanding and appreciating the rights and opinions of another person. It's about showing tolerance and decency towards the people around us – our family, friends and peers, people who are older or younger than us, people from different walks of life or who follow different cultures or religions. It also extends to physical things, such as respecting property or treating animals with care. So how can you instil respect in your child?

1 **Be a role model.** Your child is observing you constantly, and will pick up on your behaviour. What you do and say to the other people around you matters greatly.

2 **Make sure it's a two-way street.** If you treat your child with respect, you are teaching respect. Show him respect by listening to him, communicating well, and acknowledging his rights and opinions.

3 **Teach self-respect.** Children learn self-respect mostly through their interactions at home, and by being respected as loved and valued members of the family (see page 1).

4 **Be aware of morals.** Respect can't be taught in isolation, as it is part of a larger moral framework. Other positive traits, such as empathy, trust and kindness, need to be reinforced as well.

5 **Recognize fear.** Lack of respect often comes from fear. Children frequently respond to difficult situations

by playing up. Try to reassure your child and help him become more confident without resorting to being cheeky (see page 29).

6 **Show that it takes all sorts.** As your child gets older, he'll need to learn how to get along with others whose values and experiences are different from his own. Expose him to books, toys, images, TV programmes and music that promote cultural diversity.

7 **Challenge stereotypes.** Ignorance is often the reason behind lack of respect. Teach your child to become adept at spotting stereotypical or unfair images of different groups – it's vital he thinks critically about what he sees.

8 **Be compassionate.** Being compassionate means that we can see things from the point of view of others, and is a huge part of respect. Your child needs to learn that other people's feelings resemble his own. Teach him to think about what it feels like to be in someone else's shoes.

9 **Don't firefight.** Don't lecture about respect in the middle of an argument. Have conversations about respect when your child is behaving well – it's easier to get your message across and it won't feel like a personal attack.

10 **Be firm.** It's important to have firm boundaries about what constitutes respectful behaviour – for example, not damaging other people's property and not swearing. Be clear about the consequences of being disrespectful, and follow through with appropriate discipline.

Responsibility

From the tiniest toddler to the tallest teen, all children love being given responsibility. It shows that you trust them to do a job properly and that they are competent to achieve a task by themselves. Giving your child responsibility also encourages independence, problem-solving and self-confidence.

1 **Recognize real-life lessons.** Even the youngest child will learn best about responsibility from real-life situations. Looking after the family pet, remembering to do homework, packing her own school bag – these are all examples of being responsible.

2 **Be encouraging.** Encourage your child to take care of her own affairs. Children who constantly rely on their parents to remind them when they're supposed to be somewhere or what they're supposed to take will never learn responsibility.

3 **Help out.** Children soon learn that as they get older they will be expected to contribute more to the house. Chores are the perfect way for your child to learn about being a responsible member of the family (see page 21).

4 **Have fun.** Not all acts of responsibility have to be serious. Give your child the responsibility of decorating the Christmas tree, planning a family day out, choosing a gift for someone, organizing a party or preparing a surprise meal.

5 **Admit mistakes.** A big part of taking responsibility for our actions is recognizing when we've done something wrong. Encourage your child to see her mistakes as part of the learning process and to face up to them.

6 **Be true to your word.** Teach your child that when she agrees to do something, she should follow it through.

When she honours her commitments, people will take her seriously and view her as a reliable person.

7 **Don't procrastinate.** Encourage your child not to put things off. Doing things on time will help her to take control of her life and will show that she can manage her own affairs.

8 **Use your head.** People who are responsible think before they act. Encourage your child to imagine the consequences of her actions and think through different possible scenarios.

9 **Read about it.** Children can learn about responsibility through storybooks. Many children's books have a subtle moral message, such as the Harry Potter series or Luc Besson's Arthur books.

10 **Don't give too much.** You shouldn't give away too much responsibility, such as expecting your child to care for a sick adult or contribute financially to the family. Children need a childhood.

Rewards and praise

Rewards have a motivational role. They help children to see that good behaviour is valued and give parents a chance to say 'thank you' in return. Rewards come in all shapes and sizes – smiles, praise and other signs of love and approval are the best. Praise will also help your child to feel good about himself, and this is important because children who have high self-esteem are less likely to behave badly. So how can you reward and praise effectively?

1. **Act on the spot.** Reward good behaviour the moment it happens – this will help your child to make an immediate connection between behaviour and reward, and help to reinforce it.

2. **Make eye-to-eye contact.** When praising your child, get down on to his level, and use lots of eye contact, smiles and touch. This will show your child that your praise is genuine and focused.

3. **Check your tone of voice.** Think about how your voice sounds – the words might be right, but does it sound as if you are really pleased? Effective praise should be delivered spontaneously in a natural tone of voice.

4. **Be specific.** Make sure you tell your child exactly what you are praising – this will also help him make the connection between a specific behaviour and reward: for example, 'Well done for tidying your bedroom so nicely' or 'I love the colours in your painting'.

5. **Recognize the little things.** It's not always the big things that deserve the most praise. Has your child being playing quietly for a while or cleared the table without being asked? Those behaviours are just as important.

6 **Praise effort, not the end result.** If you always focus on the end result or grade, your child won't understand that what matters is how hard he tries. Rewards and praise should be for effort and commitment.

7 **Avoid mixed messages.** Mixing criticism in with words of praise is confusing and damaging. Avoid barbed comments, such as 'Well done, pity you can't do it all the time' or 'It's quite good for you'.

8 **Praise in public.** Don't be shy to praise your child in public or to tell family and friends if he has done something well. It's a thrill hearing someone say good things about you.

9 **Make reward boards.** These work well with younger children because they can see the results of their good behaviour. See Chores on page 21 for how to set up a reward chart.

10 **Teach self-evaluation.** As children get older, they still want external praise, but they also need to learn to measure how they think they've done themselves. Ask questions, such as 'How do you think you did?' or 'Are you pleased with the way your painting turned out?'

Role models

Role models are people who have a particular character or lifestyle that we want to emulate. Children tend to look up to sports stars, celebrities and fashion icons, but there's a danger that children are focusing on the wrong kinds of attributes – wealth, glamour and popularity – rather than more positive human characteristics, such as courage, talent or generosity. As a parent, you can do a lot to influence who your child chooses as a role model, but what traits should you be looking for? Here are 10 for starters.

1 **Courage.** Encourage your child to value courage as a trait. Does she know anyone who has achieved her goals against all the odds? Can she think of someone who has shown incredible bravery or strength in her daily life – someone with a disability or illness, for example?

2 **Compassion.** Can your child think of a person who has been inspirational with her kindness? Has someone given her time and money to a good cause, even when she couldn't afford to? Is she particularly charitable, altruistic or unselfish?

3 **Skill.** What about someone who is particularly talented at something? Has someone shown extraordinary skill at sport, acting, painting or music? Is she a fabulous dancer or writer? Is this role model working hard to be the best in her field?

4 **Entrepreneurship.** Children shouldn't look up to someone just because that person wealthy, but it can be positive for them to see the benefits of an entrepreneurial spirit. Is your child inspired by someone who has set up a successful business from nothing?

5 **Hard work.** Effort is everything. Children should seek role models who have shown grit, drive, perseverance and determination to achieve their goals. Does she know someone who is now reaping the rewards from years of hard work?

6 **Inventiveness.** Creative thinking is a trait to be admired. Can your child think of an inventor or scientist who changed the world with her discovery? Did someone come up with an imaginative new idea that has helped lots of people?

7 **Positivity.** What about a role model who thinks positively and enthusiastically about people and what they are capable of? Does your child know anyone who sees the good in any situation and can make the most of difficult circumstances?

8 **Knowledge.** What about someone who has a constant quest for knowledge and has dedicated his or her life to advancing human understanding? What about a role model who's good at taking knowledge and translating it to others in an inspirational or original way?

9 **Diplomacy.** Can your child think of a role model who strives to remain fair and objective under challenging circumstances? What about someone who is making it her life's work to bring peace and justice to a difficult environment? What about someone who stands up for other people?

10 **Loyalty.** Does your child know someone who is a helpful, supportive friend? Someone she can trust to be always on her side? Can she think of someone who is steadfast and faithful, even in difficult times?

Safety

As a parent, you have a million things you could worry about: abduction, major illness and drugs to name but a few. Ironically, however, the biggest threat to your child's life isn't anything so dramatic – it's everyday household accidents. Falling down stairs, scalding, poisoning from cleaning products, choking on buttons – these mundane incidents pose the greatest risk to your child's safety. At the same time, however, it's vital to allow physical and emotional freedom; you can't keep your child wrapped in cotton wool, nor should you. He needs to learn how to deal with everyday risks to become a competent adult. So how do you keep your child safe while allowing him the freedom to grow?

1   **Invest in safety gear.** If you remove needless risks from the home and stock up on safety gear, you're halfway there. Invest in the basics, such as stair gates, pond covers, smoke alarms, fireguards, cycling helmets and child locks.

2   **Provide supervision.** There's no substitute for supervision. However childproof your house is, young children should be supervised at all times. With older ones, you should take into consideration the age and abilities of each child, the activity involved, and the conditions in which it is being undertaken.

3   **Refresh your knowledge.** Rules and regulations have changed since you were a child, as have ideas about child safety. Make sure you know your stuff – the Royal Society for the Prevention of Accidents has excellent advice on its website (www.rospa.org.uk).

4   **Pass it on.** Children need to learn about safety from responsible adults, so talk to your child about risks

inside and outside the home, and how to manage them sensibly. Fun activities work better than scare tactics.

5 **Set an example.** Everyone is tempted to take short cuts, but are you sending the wrong message to your child? Do you always buckle up in the car? Do you always close the safety gate? Do you stick your knife in the toaster? Your child will copy you.

6 **Learn first aid.** Would you know how to cope in a medical emergency with your child? Are you responsible for looking after the safety of other people's children? Find a St John's Ambulance Children's First Aid course near you at www.sja.org.uk.

7 **Involve school.** Talk to your child's nursery or school about child safety classes. Are the staff planning to teach the children about preventing accidents and road safety? If not, could you organize an after-school club?

8 **Learn the three Ws.** If your child is out and about with friends, always know *where* he will be, *who* he will be with and *when* he will be back. Have a number you can contact in an emergency, whether it's a friend's house or your child's own mobile.

9 **Teach the importance of 999.** Children should always know who they can call in a dire emergency. Even the littlest fingers can dial 999.

10 **Be safe out and about.** Make sure you've got the appropriate safety belts and car seats – it's your responsibility as a parent, and it's the law. The website www.childcarseats.org.uk will help you to choose and use them properly.

Saving for the future

As noted in the 'Budgeting for family life' checklist on page 13, raising children is a costly business. For many families, the expense continues well after a child has reached 18, with parents forking out for tuition fees, driving lessons, first cars and weddings. With the increasing cost of housing, many parents are also helping their offspring to buy a home. Never mind waiting until your child leaves school, with such large sums of money involved, most parents need to think about starting a nest egg when their little ones are still in nappies. But what's the best way to save for your child's future?

1   **Clear your debts.** It's essential to pay off debts before you start saving: this is because the interest cost of debts always exceeds the interest you earn on savings. The only exception is your mortgage, which is a relatively 'cheap' way of borrowing money.

2   **Forget the biscuit barrel.** Saving money at home is not only an invitation to burglars, but your pot of cash will be worth significantly less in 18 years' time if it hasn't been earning interest.

3   **Make it little and often.** Even if you put away just a small amount of cash each month, this will grow significantly over the next 18 years. One idea is to save your weekly Child Benefit payments.

4   **Use mini-cash ISAs.** If you want to save, start with a mini-cash independent savings account (ISA). This is like a Standard Savings Account, but tax-free. At the moment you can stash up to £3000 per year.

5   **Start a Regular Savings Account.** If you want to save more than your £3000 ISA quota, consider opening a Regular Savings Account too. This requires you to pay

in a monthly amount, but gives a higher rate of interest than Standard Savings Accounts.

6 **Consider a Standard Savings Account.** If you want instant access to your savings, the next best option is a Standard Savings Account. You won't earn as much interest as with a Regular Savings Account, but it will be more than banks offer with a Current Account.

7 **Open a Children's Savings Account.** Save money in your child's name and you can put an extra £1900 in a high-interest savings account for her without paying tax on it. See www.moneysavingexpert.com for more information.

8 **Look into National Savings and Investments.** These are secure savings and investment products backed by the government. There are several options if you want to invest for your child, including Children's Bonus Bonds, Premium Bonds and Index-linked Savings Certificates. Visit www.nsandi.com for more information.

9 **Make the most of Child Trust Funds.** All babies get a free £250 voucher to open a Child Trust Fund (CTF). A further £250 is given at age seven, with children from lower income families receiving £500. Make the most of this tax-free investment opportunity.

10 **Find out about investments.** Stocks and shares, antiques, wine, art – people invest in the hope that what they lose in interest they gain in rapid appreciation. Talk to an Independent Financial Adviser (IFA) who can take you through investments of varying risks (www.searchifa.co.uk).

School trips

A handful of tragic incidents in the past few years have left both parents and teachers reluctant to let children go away with school, especially if it involves outdoor pursuits. This is a real shame, as the benefits of school trips greatly outweigh any potential risks. They provide an invaluable learning experience for children, allowing them to take part in new and exciting activities. School trips also encourage them to cooperate, explore and form friendships. So how can you reassure yourself that your child is going to be safe when he's away with his school?

1   **Know the law.** Short local trips from school do not generally require parental consent, but trips further afield require written consent from you. Make sure the school has asked your permission.

2   **Check the child-to-staff ratio.** Will there be enough staff to supervise the pupils? The requirement varies according to the number and age of the pupils, and the school is obliged to give you the regulations on this. Parents are sometimes invited to help out too, but can't be counted as trained staff.

3   **Check on staff training.** How qualified are the group leaders, especially in safety, first aid and group supervision? The website for the Royal Society for the Prevention of Accidents (www.rospa.com) has useful information about a school's duties and responsibilities towards your child.

4   **Find out about risk assessments.** Has the school carried out a risk assessment for the trip and its constituent activities? What are the significant hazards and risks? How has the school planned to avoid them? Has it consulted professional advice?

5 **Is it insured?** Check the school's insurance policy: it should cover personal injury for pupils as well as staff, public liability, medical expenses, personal effects, cancellations and special activities (particularly high-risk activities, such as outdoor pursuits).

6 **What is the total cost?** Apart from the upfront cost of the trip, there are often extra expenses, such as entrance fees, spending money and lunch money, equipment hire and special clothes. Check with the school and other parents about how much contingency money might be needed.

7 **Find out the school's travel programme.** Ask for a school trips programme for the year. If your family is on a budget, or you don't want your child to miss too many lessons, check how many trips are planned for the year – don't just go for the first one offered.

8 **Choose the most useful trips.** If you have to make a choice, ask how the trip is linked to the curriculum and how your child will benefit either educationally or socially.

9 **Know the transport arrangements.** Be sure of the plans for dropping off or picking up your child, even after a short school trip. Ask about safety belts and who will be driving.

10 **Talk to your child.** The school will brief your child, but there's no harm in reinforcing the message: listen to the group leader; don't wander off on your own; and always follow the safety instructions.

Secrets

We all know that a secret is something that you keep to yourself or share with only a few others. As children get older, they enjoy the mystery of keeping things to themselves, and it's important to allow them this independence. There are good and bad secrets, however, and it's vital that your child knows the difference between the two.

1 **Understand good secrets.** Explain to your child that good secrets don't cause harm to her or anyone else. Good secrets can also protect her from danger. Examples of a good secret are not telling someone about a surprise birthday party, or not revealing her PIN number.

2 **Recognize bad secrets.** Explain that bad secrets are ones that make her feel scared, guilty or uncomfortable. It might be something that she knows is wrong but she thinks someone will get into trouble if she tells it. No one should ever ask her to keep kisses or touches secret, for example.

3 **Be open.** Sometimes it can be hard for your child to tell which secrets are good and which are bad. Tell her that if she isn't sure, she can always ask you and you'll be honest.

4 **Be careful of promises.** Your child may only confide in you if you promise to keep the information secret. Tell her you'll do your best to help her, but don't promise to keep a secret, especially about abuse or bullying.

5 **Allow your child to share secrets.** Let your child know she can tell you anything and you won't be shocked – even if someone has made her promise not to tell, or has pressured her into keeping a secret.

6 **Respect your child's privacy.** As your child gets older, she might begin to keep a secret diary of her friendships, school life and private thoughts. Don't go snooping – she'll never forgive you.

7 **Don't share grown-up secrets.** Don't ask your child to keep secrets about negative parts of your own life, such as an affair or secret spending. The burden will be unbearable for her.

8 **Read all about it.** If you need a helping hand, the children's book *The Trouble with Secrets* by Karen Johnsen and Linda Forssell presents situations that show children when to share and when to keep a secret.

9 **Mention ChildLine.** Remind your child that she can also call ChildLine on 0800 1111 to talk about problems, including any secrets that might be worrying her and that she doesn't want to disclose to you.

10 **Tackle secretive behaviour.** It can be difficult to distinguish between normal teen behaviour and unnatural secretiveness. If you think your child is in trouble in some way, talk to her calmly. A call to Parentline Plus (0808 800 2222) will help you to negotiate the conversation.

Self-harm

Self-harm is when someone deliberately hurts or injures himself. Those who do this tend to be good at disguising their disorder, so it's difficult to be precise about the number involved. Estimates put the figure at about 10 per cent of all children, with girls being three times more likely to self-harm than boys. The reasons are not yet fully understood, but young people who self-harm have often had very difficult experiences, or use self-harm as a way of dealing with the pressures of everyday life.

It's never easy to accept the fact that someone you care about self-harms, or to understand why they do it. If you are concerned that your child might be self-harming, an organization called Young People and Self-Harm has a very useful website (www.selfharm.org.uk) that offers sound advice for friends and family. Here are the main points.

1. **Know the signs.** Self-harm can take a number of forms, including cutting, taking overdoses of tablets or medicines, punching oneself, throwing one's body against something, pulling out hair or eyelashes, scratching, picking or tearing at one's skin, causing sores and scarring, burning, and inhaling or sniffing harmful substances.

2. **Act sympathetically.** Remember that your child is extremely distressed and that self-harm may be the only way he has of communicating his feelings.

3. **Allow your child to talk.** This is probably the most important thing you can do for him. Just feeling that someone is listening and that he is finally being heard can really help. Good listening is a skill. Always let your child finish what he is saying, and while he is talking, try not to be thinking of the next thing you are going to say.

4 **Be clear and honest.** Your feelings are important too, so explain that his behaviour upsets you but that you understand it helps him to cope.

5 **Take your child seriously.** Respect his feelings, and don't tease him or call him 'mad' or 'mental'.

6 **Don't blame your child.** Try to avoid being critical, even if you feel shocked by what he is saying. This could make him feel even more alone and prevent him from talking to anyone else.

7 **Don't ask the impossible.** Avoid asking your child to promise never to self-harm. He might well do it again and then feel guilty about breaking his promise.

8 **Find someone you can talk to.** It's important that you have support as well. You should express your frustration or anger to someone other than your child.

9 **Don't blame yourself.** Your child may be self-harming for many different reasons, and it's unlikely that you will be the reason he hurts himself. Accept the fact that you can't always be there for him when he feels the need to self-harm.

10 **Consider helping in some other way.** You can do this by finding information for your child, or helping him to find a counsellor or support group. Visit www.selfharm.org.uk for more information.

Serious illness

Children are often deeply affected by the serious illness of a family member. Not only do they worry that someone they love might not get better, but they also struggle with the inevitable family stress, disrupted routines and emotional outbursts. It can be difficult to manage everyone's concerns, but as a parent, it's vital you spend time talking to your child about the illness and how the family are going to tackle it together.

1 **Don't lock them out.** Children know when something is wrong. Be honest and open about what is happening. You might think that you are protecting your child by not saying anything, but you'll only make her feel more worried.

2 **Use age-appropriate explanations.** Very young child will need to be told about the illness in simple words; for example, 'Mummy's tummy hurts' or 'Grandpa needs to have his heart mended'. Older children will appreciate more grown-up medical explanations.

3 **Talk about the prognosis.** Tell your child what will happen during the illness and the possible plan of treatment. Reassure her that the doctors are doing everything they can.

4 **Take your child on hospital visits.** Let your child visit whenever possible. This will demystify the whole business of hospitals, doctors and illness. It will also be good for your child to have contact with her loved one.

5 **Alleviate worries.** Your child might think that she somehow caused the illness by misbehaving or not doing well at school. Make sure she knows this isn't true.

6 **Be aware of sibling rivalry.** A healthy child might be jealous of a poorly sibling who is getting lots of attention. Listen to her concerns and try to spend special 'alone time' with her. Reassure her with lots of love and kisses.

7 **'What will happen to me?'** Children naturally worry about their own health. Your child may also be frightened about who will take care of her if the worst happens. Let her know that she will always be loved and cared for.

8 **Be as normal as possible.** Try to keep a normal routine at home and school. Children like to have order. It will make your child feel safe and secure to know what will happen each day.

9 **Don't let her take on too much.** With one pair of hands in hospital, the rest of the family has to take up the strain. Just make sure that your child isn't over-burdened with chores, schoolwork and hospital visits. She may feel bad about not coping.

10 **Consider family counselling.** If the prognosis looks bad, or your child is struggling to cope, consider family therapy. It might help your child to express her fears and anger in a no-blame environment.

Sex education

It used to be thought that the earlier you talked to children about sex, the sooner they would engage in sexual activity. The reality is actually the opposite. Children who are fully armed with appropriate and accurate sex education are more likely to *delay* having sex; they are also more likely to use contraception and less likely to fall victim to sexually transmitted diseases or teenage pregnancy. But how do you talk to your child about sex and what is appropriate? The UK government has this advice for parents.

1 **Start when your child is small.** Encourage him to ask questions, and answer them simply.

2 **Make it part of everyday life.** Talking about sex should not be just a one-off conversation, so keep an open dialogue going as your child gets older.

3 **Start early.** Introduce the topic before your child reaches puberty, as waiting until then can make it awkward.

4 **Ask his opinion.** Ask your child how he feels about different situations to find out how much he knows already. You can then give him answers and advice that he can understand.

5 **Use the media.** Soaps, adverts, TV programmes and magazines are all good ways of getting a conversation going. Your child might find it easier to discuss sex if it's in relation to someone else.

6 **Use books, leaflets and websites.** These can be really useful if you need information or ideas on how to start talking. Call Parentline Plus free on 0808 800 2222 to talk in confidence. The Family Planning Association

can also provide information and advice. Their helpline number is 0845 310 1334.

7 Give your child privacy. As your child grows, he will need privacy, and might not always want to talk to you. For advice on sex, relationships and contraception, young people under 18 years old can call Sexwise on 0800 28 29 30. Calls are confidential and free of charge from landlines.

8 Talk about feelings. It's important for your child to consider the feelings of others in relationships, not just the biology.

9 Be open-minded. Keep talking to your child, even if you are shocked by his attitudes and values.

10 Talk to other parents. Find out how they answer difficult questions and discuss difficult issues.

Shyness

All children, particularly young ones, show a degree of shyness when presented with people and situations that are unfamiliar. If your child's shyness becomes so overwhelming that it starts to interfere with her school life or social life, however, it's time for you to step in. Left alone, chronically shy children often go on to become socially awkward adults, missing out on meaningful relationships and life opportunities that other people take for granted.

1 **Recognize that shyness is natural.** If your child has had little or no contact with others, either through choice or circumstance, starting a new school or nursery will be tough. Ask your education provider to ease her in with gentle 'settling-in' sessions.

2 **Is self-image the problem?** Children hate feeling different. Is your child shy about her hair or skin colour, a disability, being over- or underweight, tall or short, or facing puberty especially early? Use the 'Confidence and self-esteem' checklist on page 29 to help.

3 **Be a role model.** If parents lack confidence, this fear is often passed down to their children. Is it time to tackle your own social demons? Consider attending a confidence workshop or taking a brief course of cognitive behavioural therapy to retrain your approach to public situations.

4 **Consider your own behaviour.** Children often develop shyness as a response to having domineering, aggressive or overly gregarious parents. Is your child retreating into herself because she can't compete with another family member?

5 **Check for bullying.** Public humiliation, especially in the form of bullying, can have a devastating effect on a

child's confidence. See the 'Bullying' checklist on page 15 if you think this may be behind your child's shyness.

6 **Discourage unhelpful comments.** Watch out for unhelpful, 'amusing' or hurtful remarks made by family members in passing. School reports, exam results, sporting success (or lack of it) are all hot topics for ridicule. Is a relative unwittingly undermining your child's self-image?

7 **Is your child embarrassed?** Children face the world on behalf of their family, especially at school. If parents split up, have a different culture or disabilities, are in prison, or are just a bit different, children can feel ashamed and shy. Encourage your child to share her worries. A quick word with her teacher might also bring in extra support.

8 **Find a hypnotherapist.** Hypnotherapy can work for some people by helping them to alter their feelings and behaviour. It's also been shown to be effective against blushing, one of the most obvious signs of shyness. Find a practitioner near you at www.hypnotherapistregister.com.

9 **Avoid isolating activities.** Shyness can become a self-fulfilling prophecy. Children who are shy tend to choose lone activities, such as watching TV or playing computer games, which then isolate them further from other children. Gently nudge your child towards more social activities, such as drama, sport, crafts or music.

10 **Consider counselling.** Pathological shyness is a form of social anxiety. A trained therapist will be able to help your child focus on what has caused her shyness and suggest ways to improve her social confidence. Talk to your family GP about a referral.

Siblings

Despite being brought up together, brothers and sisters can have wildly varying temperaments and personalities. As a parent, it can be difficult to manage these differences: you want your children to express their different personalities, but you'd also like them to get on under the same roof. Age makes a huge difference too – how can you ensure that older and younger siblings relate to each other in a harmonious way? It's not always easy, but here are some golden rules to get you started.

1 **Do not make comparisons.** Siblings feel frustrated if parents compare one child unfavourably with another. This can also lead to low self-esteem and resentment. Praise your child for accomplishments in relation to himself, not in comparison to a sibling.

2 **Avoid labels.** People who are pigeon-holed as children tend to carry these narrow roles into adulthood. Labelling your child as 'the sporty one' or 'the clever one' also leads to sibling rivalry, and doesn't take into account your child's complex achievements.

3 **Help your child be someone to look up to.** Older children can act as surrogate parents, steering youngsters away from danger, defending them at school, or talking to them when they're upset. Praising older siblings when they act responsibly will foster good relationships in the family.

4 **Develop cooperation.** Encourage siblings to cooperate. Give brothers and sisters tasks that require them to work together for a shared goal. If they wash the car together, for example, the prize could be a joint trip to the cinema.

5 **Foster team spirit.** Blood is thicker than water. Feeling part of a family is a great way to promote

harmony amongst siblings. Enjoy sports as a family, work out problems as a family, and play games as a family.

6 **Know when to step back.** Siblings should handle small disagreements by themselves. Tell them what you expect: for example, 'Learn to share the toy nicely or neither of you will be allowed to play with it.' This shows that you want them to work out the conflict themselves, and there'll be consequences if they don't.

7 **Know when to step in.** While some disagreements can be sorted out between siblings, you need to know when to step in. Make sure your children know that you will not tolerate verbal or physical attacks between them.

8 **Ensure equality.** Children don't have to be treated equally. It's not realistic or desirable to treat your children exactly the same, but while smaller children get the benefits of being 'babied', older children should enjoy privileges and more responsibilities as they grow.

9 **Have no favourites.** Don't fall into the 'Who's best?' trap. If your child asks you, remember that he doesn't actually expect you to say who's better; he's just fishing for reassurance about how you feel about him.

10 **Watch out for stepchildren and adopted or foster children.** They may already feel unsure about their position in the family, and their relationship with other siblings could cause problems if both are not treated fairly and sensitively. Talk to Parentline Plus (0808 800 2222) if you're feeling out of your depth.

Sleep and bedtimes

To understand why sleep is so important you only have to look at what happens when you don't get enough. Long-term sleep deprivation causes all manner of problems – lack of concentration, mood swings, lowered immunity, slowed reaction times and memory loss to name but a few. It's also been linked to more surprising conditions, such as obesity and raised blood pressure. It's vital, therefore, that our children get a good night's sleep, but just how many hours do they need?

Below you'll see the recommended number of hours' sleep that a child needs per day, including daytime naps for toddlers. These figures are only approximations. The best indicator that your child is getting enough sleep is if she looks rested and healthy in the morning, and isn't feeling sleepy during school hours.

Note: Bedtimes are calculated on the child waking at 7.00 a.m.

1   **Age 2.** Your child needs roughly 13 hours of sleep per day, including a nap around lunchtime. Recommended bedtime in the evening is 6.30.

2   **Age 3.** Your child needs 12 hours of sleep per day, including a nap around lunchtime. Recommended bedtime in the evening is 7.30.

3   **Age 4.** Your child needs to get all her 11.5 hours of sleep at night, as she won't be able to nap at school. Recommended bedtime in the evening is 7.30.

4   **Age 5–6.** Your child needs around 11 hours of sleep. Recommended bedtime in the evening is 8.00.

5   **Ages 7–8.** Your child needs around $10^1/_2$ hours of sleep at night. Recommended bedtime in the evening is 8.30.

6   **Ages 8–9.** Your child needs around 10 hours of sleep at night. Recommended bedtime in the evening is 9.00.

7 **Ages 10–11.** Your child needs around nine and a half hours of sleep at night. Recommended bedtime in the evening is 9.30.

8 **Ages 12–14.** By secondary school, your child will manage on nine hours a night. Recommended bedtime in the evening is 10.00.

9 **Ages 15–16.** Your child needs around eight and a half hours a night. Recommended bedtime in the evening is 10.30.

10 **Age 17 and over.** By this age your child will have long been dictating his own bedtime. However, the current guidelines still suggest eight hours a night and a bedtime of 11.00 p.m.

Smoking

It's staggering to think that around 450 children take up smoking each day in the UK. Equally horrifying is that by the age of 15, one in four teens is a regular smoker. Children who smoke often go on to become adult smokers, and thus face all the health risks that this entails. But perhaps less well known is how many children suffer from the immediate health consequences from smoking. Children who regularly puff away are much more susceptible to coughs, colds, wheeziness and shortness of breath. They're also more likely to take more time off school. So how do you stop your child from smoking?

1 **Set an example.** Children whose parents smoke are four times more likely to become smokers. It's easy to blame peer pressure, but actually stopping yourself can greatly influence whether your child takes up the habit.

2 **Explain about addiction.** Children who experiment with cigarettes quickly become addicted. Talk about addiction – explain that smoking is not something you can just take or leave; it's potentially a habit that will continue throughout life.

3 **Encourage individuality.** Most young smokers are influenced by their friends' smoking habits, and can often feel pressured into taking that first puff. Praise your child for following his own path, and encourage him to be confident within his own choices (see page 29).

4 **Discuss, don't dictate.** A blanket disapproval of smoking can often make it seem more alluring. Give your child the facts and he's more likely to stick to a decision he feels is his.

5 **Share experiences.** Watching a parent or family friend go through the difficultly of stopping smoking can

greatly influence a child's attitude. Observing how hard it is to stop can put more significance on what smoking 'just one cigarette' really means.

6 **Find something your child can relate to.** The threat of lung cancer doesn't carry much weight with a 13-year-old. Discuss side effects that will strike a chord with young people, such as bad skin, smelly breath, impotence, or the inability to participate in sports.

7 **Calculate the cost.** Smoking is expensive, and the price is going up every year. It's a simple calculation to work out how much 10 cigarettes a day will cost over a 10-year period – your child will soon work out that's a lot of pocket money.

8 **Don't overreact if your child is smoking.** Even if you are disappointed at this discovery, talk to your child in a non-confrontational manner. Find out about the reasons why he started smoking so that you'll be in a better position to advise him.

9 **Offer to help.** Accompany your child to your local NHS stop smoking service, which can provide group or one-to-one counselling and medication. Focus on the positives and praise any progress he makes with giving up the habit.

10 **Get more information.** Find your local NHS stop smoking service by visiting www.gosmokefree.co.uk, where you can also get useful information on making your home a smoke-free zone.

Specific learning difficulties

One of the most frustrating things about specific learning difficulties (SpLDs) is that they regularly go undiagnosed. There are four main SpLDs:

Dyslexia is a learning difficulty with literacy. Reading, memory, speed of processing, sequencing skills and spoken language can often be affected.

Dyscalculia is a learning difficulty with numbers. Children may also have difficulty telling the time, calculating prices and measuring.

Dyspraxia causes children to find balance, coordination and handling objects difficult. Writing and pronunciation may also be affected, and there may be an over- or under-sensitivity to noise, light and touch.

Attention Deficit Disorder (ADD) causes children to have a very short attention span and be easily distracted. The hyper-activity that often accompanies this condition can make children act impulsively and erratically.

As a parent, it is essential to find out where to get help and what can be done to assist your child both at home and school. Here are some starting points.

1   **Trust your instinct.** Parents know their children better than anyone. If you have a gut feeling that your child has an undiagnosed SpLD, seek help immediately.

2   **Do your homework.** Knowledge is power when it comes to getting help for your child. It will be a big help if you can understand her specific struggles.

3   **Talk to your GP.** If your child is too young to be at school, talk to your doctor or health visitor. They will be able to offer you advice about getting your child assessed.

4   **Take early action.** If your child is at pre-school or primary school, talk to her class teacher, the special educational needs coordinator (SENCO), or the head teacher.

5   **Seek help for older children too.** If your child is at secondary school, contact his form teacher, the SENCO, head of year or head teacher.

6   **Take the matter further.** If, after talking to the school, you still feel your child has difficulties that have not been identified, ask the Local Education Authority to carry out a statutory assessment of her special educational needs.

7   **Work together.** The closer you work with your child's teachers, the more successful any help for your child can be.

8   **Join a support group.** As well as providing the chance to meet other parents and children coping with SpLDs, support groups are often great sources of information and advice. They also tend to have access to the latest research on your child's condition.

9   **Be positive.** Look for the upside. Dyslexic children, for example, often have good visuo-spatial skills, creativity and intuition. Who'd have thought that Jamie Oliver, Noel Gallagher, Tom Cruise, Richard Branson and Albert Einstein all have dyslexia in common?

10 **Boost confidence.** Your child may have an SpLD, but it doesn't define who she is. Make sure she has lots of opportunities to boost her self-esteem and show off the things she is good at.

Spirituality

The first point to make here is that spirituality is not the same as religion. While spirituality can certainly be expressed through a religion or an affiliation to a faith community, it's not the only way. In the context of this book spirituality refers to the need for children to be able to express their inbuilt curiosity about the world, to ask questions about the meaning of life and what happens after death. Spirituality is ultimately about connecting with something greater than ourselves, whether that feeling is connected to nature, to other human beings or to a higher power. So how can you encourage your child to think about such complex and far-reaching ideas?

1 **Make time to talk.** In the rush of modern life, parents and children rarely get time to sit down together and share their thoughts and feelings about wider issues. Make time for relaxed discussions about dreams, ideas and speculations.

2 **Don't tease.** Children are naturally drawn to magical ideas about fairies, witches, ghosts and other fantasy figures. Don't be too quick to disillusion your child, as these characters can be a great source of comfort and creativity.

3 **Discuss faith and religion.** Whether you have a faith or not, it's important that your child learns about other belief systems. Children who engage in critical discussions about religious and philosophical ideas become more tolerant, open-minded adults.

4 **Encourage a love of books.** Children adore stories about magic, mystery and fantasy. Far from being nonsense, these books often help children to learn about more complicated notions, such as self-belief, hope, life and death, good and evil, and courage.

5 **Embrace the big questions.** Don't shy away from big questions: 'What happens when I die?' 'Who made all the animals?' 'Are there such things as ghosts?' Parents often dread these posers, but don't worry – you're not supposed to have all the answers. Just be honest. Talk about your beliefs, while reminding your child that other people hold different views.

6 **Explore different options.** As children grow and develop their own ideas, they'll answer the big questions for themselves. As a parent, the best thing you can do is expose your child to lots of differing opinions and let him make up his own mind.

7 **Appreciate the world.** Many people find spirituality in the beauty and power of nature. Encourage your child to love the outdoors – let him walk in the rain, play in the snow, enjoy sunsets, ponder the stars, see magnificent views and listen to thunderstorms.

8 **Don't focus on material things.** Whether you're a humanist or a Hindu, the key to spirituality is the idea that it's what's inside that counts.

9 **Enjoy multi-faith celebrations.** In modern Britain our children will mix and make friends with children from a great variety of religious and cultural backgrounds. Whether it's Passover or St Patrick's Day, don't be afraid to celebrate and share this diversity with your child.

10 **It's OK not to know.** Children like certainties. Part of developing a spiritual self is to recognize that sometimes it's OK not to have all the answers. Teach your child to feel comfortable with the idea that, as humans, we always have more to learn.

Sport

What's the difference between exercise and sport? While exercise can refer to any activity that maintains fitness, a sport has the added element of rules or customs, and is often engaged in competitively. Aerobics is exercise, for example, while rugby is a sport. All types of exercise are important for the physical and emotional well-being of your child, but taking part in a sport will often give her the chance to learn about important social values, such as leadership and cooperation. So how do you get your child fired up about sports?

1 **Attend sporting events.** Nothing beats the excitement of live sport, so take your child to lots of different sporting events – from village cricket matches to Olympic races – and let her soak up the atmosphere.

2 **Show your enthusiasm.** Children often pick up sporting interests from a friend or family member. If you have a sporting passion, don't be afraid to share it with your child; it might become a wonderful joint pursuit.

3 **Turn off the TV.** Discourage sedentary pursuits for your child. Put time limits on the use of computers and televisions, as these always compete with more active pursuits.

4 **Play sports together as a family.** From cricket on the beach to football in the park, there are lots of games you can enjoy as a family. Just don't make it too competitive or you'll turn off your child's interest.

5 **Make sport for all.** More boys than girls take part in sports, perhaps because culturally we encourage girls to be more restrained and less active. From the word go, it's vital that parents teach girls to enjoy the rough and tumble of physical play.

6 **Show your support.** Encourage your child's sporting endeavours. Make a real effort to attend as many school sports days and team matches as possible. Praise her, even if she comes fourth in the sack race.

7 **Get involved.** Ask the school if there are ways you can help with after-school sports, such as coaching or refereeing. If you don't have any specific sporting skills, you can still support the team by offering transport or half-time refreshments.

8 **Let children choose.** Your child will only stick at a sport of her choosing. The best thing you can do is to present a variety of options, help her find equipment, and offer lots of encouragement.

9 **Nurture talent.** If your child shows talent, you might want to think about a specialist secondary school or sports academy that encourages this. Local sports clubs also offer opportunities for gifted youngsters to play in junior teams and receive coaching.

10 **Go solo sometimes.** If your child hates team games, think of a sport she can do on her own, or ones that are not competitive. Cycling, skating, swimming, skate-boarding or gymnastics can be done solo or with a friend or parent.

Starting school

The move from pre-school to proper school is a daunting prospect. For little children, it's a whole new world of sights, smells and sounds, as well as a bewildering mix of potential friends and teachers. For parents, it's an emotional watershed because starting school is your child's first step away from the apron strings and towards independence. So how can you make it easier for everyone involved?

1 **Prepare your child.** A school-age child needs to know how to go to the toilet unaided, how to dress himself and feel confident enough to speak to other children and adults. The website www.raisingchildren.co.uk has details of the skills your child should have before he starts school.

2 **Make the school a familiar place.** Before your child starts, go past the building every day. Talk about how the children there are having fun and how *you* enjoyed school. Read some inspiring, positive stories with him about school, such as *Starting School* by Allan and Janet Ahlberg.

3 **Visit the school yourself.** Find the answers to any questions you have, including what your child needs on his first day of school, what the school day entails, and lunch arrangements. Is there an open day?

4 **Make friends.** If you know the parents of any children starting at the same time, why not set up a pre-school play-date a few weeks before term? Starting school with a few friends will help your child to feel more confident.

5 **Check the travelling time.** Walk or drive the route to check how long it takes. Always allow extra time once you start taking your child to school – you don't want to raise his anxiety levels by rushing or arriving late.

6 **Get into the routine.** Most children start school in September after a summer of playing outside and late nights. Prepare them for school by gradually making bedtime and waking-up time fit in with the school routine. Have meals at set times too.

7 **Follow the settling-in programmes.** These are operated by most schools. Your child will go with you to look around and meet the teacher, then go for one or more half days each week to get used to the school routine and fellow classmates.

8 **Find out about school uniforms.** If there's a school uniform, buy it well in advance to make sure you have everything ready for the first day. Don't forget any indoor pumps, name tags and sports kit that your child might need.

9 **Be organized.** Have a checklist of what your child needs every day for school, and remind yourself about keeping up with clean uniforms. Have fresh, healthy items ready in the fridge if he takes a packed lunch.

10 **Control your emotions.** Saying goodbye can be difficult, but it's important to be all smiles. Reassure your child that you'll pick him up at the end of school, give him a hug and leave. Most children have a little cry at this point, but it soon passes. Chances are he'll enjoy himself so much that he won't want to come home!

Stranger danger

Despite the fact that you want to protect your child, it's impossible to be together all the time. It's vital that your child is savvy about 'stranger danger'. She needs to know how to stay safe and protect herself from uncomfortable or potentially life-threatening situations with people she doesn't know. Here are 10 ways to keep your child from harm.

1 **Be clear about what a stranger is.** Children often have distorted ideas about what a stranger might look like, expecting the person to be ugly or frightening. Be clear to your child that a stranger is absolutely anyone – male or female, young or old – that she does not know.

2 **Stay cool.** Talk calmly about the problem of stranger danger and why it's important to stay safe. Be careful not to alarm your child unduly and make her worry excessively about dangers in the world.

3 **Know your audience.** Talk about things in an age-appropriate way. Little children might benefit most from stories or role-play, while older children will respond to more grown-up conversations and real-life examples.

4 **Spot the ploy.** Teach your child to spot typical ploys used by strangers to entice children away from safety: for example, offering sweets or lifts home in a car, or helping to find a lost puppy or kitten.

5 **Practise what to say.** Make a game out of posing different scenarios: for example, 'What would you do if someone asks you to get in their car and says your mummy said it was OK?' Work out the correct plan of action together.

6 **Be aware that not all secrets are safe.** If an older child or adult has pressurized your child into keeping

a secret, it could lead to danger. Make sure she knows the difference between good and bad secrets (see page 137).

7 **Know the three Ws.** Always know *where* your child will be, *who* she'll be with and *when* she'll be home. Agree who will be picking her up and stick to it.

8 **Explain who to approach.** If your child gets lost, she might need to get help from a stranger. In this case, tell her to seek out a shop assistant, a mum with a child, or a police officer. She can also walk into safe places, such as a library or a doctor's surgery.

9 **Be as noisy as possible.** Children spend most of their lives being told not to make a scene in public. Make it clear that if your child ever feels threatened, it's OK to yell, kick, punch, scream, shout or run away from an adult.

10 **Get the school involved.** Many police forces are happy to send an officer to schools to explain about stranger danger. If your school doesn't have such an event planned, talk to a teacher or the Parent Teacher Association (PTA) about arranging one.

Swearing

Children swear for all sorts of reasons. They hear adults using bad language, so it makes them feel more grown up to use it themselves. Children also understand the power of swear words; they see that bad language gets a response from parents, whether it's anger, shock or laughter. Most children know that cursing is wrong, and use it to feel rebellious and accepted by their peer group. What children often don't understand, however, is why swearing is unacceptable in most situations. That's where you come in.

1 Explain. Tell your child why swearing is wrong. Swear words are insulting and abusive. Their purpose is to denigrate and hurt the listener. Many swear words are also discriminatory, in that they pick out a specific social group for ridicule.

2 Set clear limits. Rules are most effective if they're explained in a calm way. Make sure your child knows that swear words are not acceptable. Outline the future consequences for bad language, and be consistent.

3 Make one rule for all. If you want your child not to swear, it's important that the whole family plays by the same rules. Wipe out any name calling or swearing at home.

4 Monitor yourself. As hard as you try, you might let the odd swear word slip out in front of your child. Always apologize – it shows consistency in your approach to bad language.

5 Don't laugh. It's wrong to laugh when your toddler uses 'naughty' words. He might say them again to see you smile, rather than understanding that they are not to be used. Explain that, as a family, you don't use those words, and ignore him if he tries it out again.

6 **Recognize that children copy.** If you use a particular word when angry, your child might say this swear word when very distressed or angry with you or his peers. Try to get him to explain his feelings properly, understand the distress and clear up the problem rather than fussing about the word used.

7 **Make up a family word.** If you want to express frustration or anger, make up a word (preferably a nonsense word or something uncontroversial) to use instead of swearing.

8 **Explain sexual swear words.** If an older child uses sexual swear words, he might be embarrassed to hear what they actually mean, and that could be enough to stop him using them. In any case, explain that they are offensive and inappropriate.

9 **Use humour.** If your child needs to find a word to use when he's upset or angry, encourage him to choose something funny. With any luck, it will make him laugh and help diffuse the situation.

10 **Get the school involved.** Many children watch their Ps and Qs at home, but this is often not the case with friends in the playground. Make sure school has a no-tolerance policy towards swearing.

Tantrums

It happens overnight. Without a word of warning, your happy, smiley toddler turns into a tiny tearaway. This difficult period starts any time from nine months onwards and can reduce even the steeliest of parents to shreds. The good news is that tantrums are not about disobedience, but simple frustration: your child gets worked up at not being able to do or communicate what she wants. This is not the time for naughty steps and 10-point behaviour star charts. By all means be firm and clear about what is and isn't acceptable, but what your child really needs is help in dealing with the storm of emotions that's spinning her out of control.

1. **Don't overdo it.** A tired, hungry child is a tantrum waiting to happen. Stick to regular mealtimes and bedtimes.

2. **Make your house safe.** If all you ever say is 'Don't touch that', you're inviting rebellion.

3. **Anticipate frustration.** Step in and help when your child has taken on a challenge too far. Remember that loud noises, new people, strange places and scary situations can also trigger tantrums in young children

4. **Get up a little earlier.** Mornings are the peak tantrum time and parental patience wears thin in the dash to get to work, the nursery or the shops. Give yourself a few extra minutes to save tempers all round.

5. **Use distraction.** When the bottom lip starts to wobble, point to a bird in the garden, a car in the street, a toy over the other side of the room – anything that will divert your child's attention.

6. **Act the fool.** She won't get in the buggy? You get in instead! Laughing at silly old Mummy or Daddy is a great way to break the tension.

7 **Hold tight.** Screaming children can often be scared by their emotions. Holding your child firmly can help her keep it together.

8 **Count to 10.** Seeing your child throw a tantrum can make you anxious, bewildered or angry. Take time to regain your cool, but also stick to your guns. Don't give in or your child will learn that tantrums work.

9 **Hug when it's over.** Don't lecture, punish or ask for apologies. Your child's been through enough. Give her a cuddle and move on.

10 **Don't make a scene.** If you're in a public place, take your child to another room, a quiet corner or the car park until she's calmed down.

Teenage pregnancy

Britain has one of the highest teenage birth rates in the developed world. The reasons behind this are not entirely understood, but most experts blame the British culture of secrecy and embarrassment about sex, combined with inadequate sex education at an early age. While teenage girls can cope physically with the biological demands of pregnancy, giving birth at a young age is strongly associated with disadvantages in later life; teen mums are twice as likely to live in poverty and be without a partner in their 30s.

1 **Get talking.** Research shows that teenage girls are less likely to become pregnant if they feel comfortable talking about sex and relationships with their parents.

2 **Liaise with the school.** Find out what sex education your child is getting at school. If you think it's inadequate, talk to the head teacher or approach the board of governors.

3 **Fill the gaps.** Provide your child with information and advice on the subjects not covered at school, such as feelings, peer pressure, relationships, self-esteem and love.

4 **Give moral support.** Offer to go with your daughter to the doctor or sexual health clinic to discuss any issues about contraception. She might be too embarrassed to go by herself.

5 **Ensure awareness of STIs.** Some 25 per cent of teens believe the pill protects against sexually transmitted infections (STIs). Make sure your teenager has all the facts and knows how to stay safe.

6 **Offer further help.** Point your daughter child towards www.ruthinking.co.uk, an excellent website for teens

that contains information about sex, contraception, pregnancy and STIs.

7 **Consider your response to a teenage pregnancy.** Your first reaction is likely to be shock and despair. Try to stay cool and talk through the options; your child will be in a state of emotional turmoil and will need time and your help to come to a rational decision.

8 **Seek professional advice.** If your daughter thinks she is pregnant, confirm the pregnancy with your GP or local health clinic. There are usually services in the area for pregnant teenagers, both in hospitals and the community, beyond routine antenatal care. These include counsellors who will be able to give your daughter impartial advice on her options.

9 **Talk to the school.** Some schools encourage pregnant pupils to continue their studies; others aren't so progressive. If there's no joy with school, consider home tuition. The Education Department of your local council will be able to help.

10 **Find out the father's responsibility.** All birth parents have a legal duty to support their child financially, even if they don't have parental responsibility. If your daughter applies to the Child Support Agency (CSA) for child maintenance, and the alleged father denies parentage, the CSA can take action to determine if he is the father of that child, including a DNA test.

Teeth

There's nothing nicer than a healthy set of gnashers. A lovely smile with sparkling teeth looks great and will give your child bags of confidence. More importantly, his teeth will help him eat, chew and talk properly. They'll also give his face structure and support. As a parent, there's lots you can do to help your child keep his teeth in tip-top condition.

1 **Know what to expect and when.** All the milk teeth should be through by age three. By six, your child should start to lose his milk teeth and grow permanent teeth. By 14, he will have all his permanent teeth, apart from wisdom teeth, which come later.

2 **Make friends with your dentist.** Don't wait until your child has a toothache. Find a dentist who is great with children, and make sure your child visits regularly. The dentist will be able to tell you how to brush your toddler's teeth, or show an older child how to do it himself.

3 **Take free treatment.** Children are treated free under the NHS, so take advantage while you can. To find an NHS dentist in your area, go to www.bda-findadentist.org.uk or phone NHS Direct on 0845 4647.

4 **Brush twice a day.** Children's teeth need brushing morning and night with a children's toothpaste (don't use your own as this will have too much fluoride in it). If your child is under the age of seven, he should be supervised to make sure he is cleaning properly.

5 **Use the right toothbrush.** A child's toothbrush needs to be soft and small enough to use comfortably. Bright colours, favourite characters, brushes that play a tune – all these will be attractive to your child and make a mundane routine fun.

6 **Keep sugary food to mealtimes.** It's not just the quantity of sugar eaten that is the problem, but how often. Don't allow sugary snacks between meals. Processed toddler foods can also contain quite a lot of sugar, so always read the label.

7 **Limit fizzy drinks.** Make sure your child drinks lots of water instead of fizzy drinks and sugary juices. Fizzy drinks, including diet ones, are acidic and cause rapid erosion of the teeth.

8 **End a meal with milk.** You can help to protect against tooth erosion by finishing a meal with an alkaline food or drink, such as cheese or milk. This will neutralize the acid in your child's mouth.

9 **Have lots of vitamin C.** Make sure your child gets plenty of fruit and vegetables that contain vitamin C, as it promotes healthy teeth and gums and aids the absorption of iron.

10 **Stock up on calcium.** Calcium is vital for healthy teeth. Milk and dairy products are great sources, as are soya beans, tofu and fish that has edible bones (such as sardines, whitebait and pilchards).

Television

Television has transformed our lives. Never before have children had access to such a variety of images and opinions. While many of these programmes are wonderfully educational and entertaining, the vast majority of television programming is not aimed at children and therefore may not be suitable. Left to their own devices, children will watch almost anything, so it's up to parents to guard the goggle-box.

1 **Be the judge.** As a parent, it's your responsibility to judge the suitability of your child's viewing. Unless she is watching programmes specifically made for a young audience, it's important to try to watch with her so that you can monitor and explain as you go.

2 **Get talking.** Talk to your child about her viewing habits. TV can be a great conversation starter for difficult topics, such as teenage pregnancy, smoking, drugs or bullying.

3 **Be wise to adverts.** Don't let your child get sucked in by children's advertising. Teach her to distinguish between a programme and an advert. It's important for her to learn that adverts present things in an unreal or idealistic way.

4 **Check programme ratings.** They're there for a good reason: to give parents advance warning of any content that may be unsuitable or upsetting for children. The same goes for the 9 p.m. watershed: anything shown after that time is generally considered unsuitable for children.

5 **Protect your PIN.** If you have digital TV, make sure you need a PIN to access pay-per-view and adult content. Do not give your child access to this PIN.

6 **Set the rules.** Don't be afraid to set clear limits for your child's viewing habits. Include how many hours she is allowed to watch and what kinds of programmes are suitable.

7 **Share concerns.** It's no use banning certain programmes if your child watches them at a friend's house. Check with the other parents if you suspect this is happening, and try to agree a joint approach.

8 **Keep TV out of the bedroom.** Three hours of TV a day has been shown to cause sleep disorders in children, so limit your child's watching habits and don't let her have a TV in her bedroom. It's also difficult to control your child's viewing habits if she has a set in her own space.

9 **Don't have the TV on in the background.** The flashing picture and noise can distract even the youngest toddler from concentrating on play or homework. Children need to learn to focus and concentrate on what they are doing.

10 **Avoid couch potato children.** Watch out for the connection between TV and obesity. Children who eat their meals in front of the television are more prone to overeating and less likely to burn off the calories with physical activity.

Toilet training

You wouldn't believe how competitive parents can get about potty training, believing that the younger a child is toilet trained, the better. In recent studies by developmental paediatricians, however, findings suggest that potty training any younger than 27 months is simply too early. Toddlers under this age find potty training tough going, and it can take a long time for any change in behaviour to take hold. After 27 months, on the other hand, it seems generally to take less time and stress to complete.

1   **Look for the signs.** Your child may be ready to start potty training if he stays dry for a few hours each day, takes an interest when you go to the toilet, has regular bowel movements, and lets you know when his nappy is soiled.

2   **Pick a good time.** Don't start potty training during a period of stress or upheaval, such as a new baby, starting nursery or moving house. Your child will be too distracted.

3   **Leave a potty lying around.** Get a potty a few weeks before you suggest your child uses it. Leave it around for your child to discover by himself. He might try sitting on it fully clothed, or put his teddy in it.

4   **Choose potty spots.** If you want, you can have more than one potty around the house so that your child doesn't have far to go. Always try to place the potty on a hard surface where spills will be easier to clean away.

5   **Try sitting without a nappy.** Once your child has got used to the presence of a potty, try letting him sit on it without a nappy. If you're lucky, he might do something. If not, be patient – potty training can take weeks, if not months. It'll happen eventually.

6   **Be positive.** Praise any positive result. If he manages to do a wee or a poo, tell him how clever he is. Chances are you might get a repeat performance the next time.

7   **Provide suitable clothes.** Forget clothes with lots of buttons or fasteners. Your toddler needs stretchy clothing that's easy to pull up and down in a hurry.

8   **Don't force.** Avoid getting cross about accidents, and never force your toddler to sit on a potty. It's also important not to show disgust at the contents of the bowl, otherwise you'll discourage any future efforts.

9   **Make it easy for yourself.** Place a few sheets of loo paper in the bottom of the potty – it'll make it much easier to tip the contents down the loo and clean out afterwards.

10   **Ensure basic hygiene.** Potties should be stored clean and dry. After each use, empty the contents of the potty into the toilet, wipe it and disinfect it. Make sure you and your child always wash your hands.

Truancy

Every day 50,000 schoolchildren play truant. If you think your child might be one of those, it's worth knowing that children who truant not only fall behind academically, but also miss out on friendships and the other social benefits of school. As a parent, you have a legal responsibility to make sure your child attends classes, so what can you do to keep both her and you on the right side of the law? Here are 10 tips to tackle truancy.

1 **Take it seriously.** Parents are committing an offence if they fail to ensure their child's regular attendance at school. You could face a fine of up to £2500, a prison sentence of up to three months or a community sentence.

2 **Make your views clear.** Truanters often claim that their parents don't mind if they miss school. Ensure that your child knows how important school is and that you definitely do not approve of her missing lessons.

3 **Check for bullying.** A large proportion of children miss school because of fear of bullying. If this is the underlying problem, use the 'Bullying' checklist on page 15 to get help immediately.

4 **Find out how your child is getting on.** Very bright children sometimes skip school through boredom, while those who are struggling simply can't face classes. Could problems with schoolwork be at the root of your child's absence?

5 **Get them there on time.** Is your child consistently late for school? Make sure she gets up, leaves the house and arrives at school on time. You might have to drop her off yourself to make sure.

6 **Avoid term-time trips.** Don't take your child on holiday in term-time. If she loses just two weeks' education every year, over 10 years it adds up to the same as one entire year of schooling.

7 **Be interested.** Children like to feel their efforts are rewarded. Praise your child for her achievements at school, however small, and always take an active interest in her day (see page 67).

8 **Book appointments for after school.** Emergency visits to the doctor or dentist can't be helped, but always try to schedule routine check-ups, vaccinations and other non-emergency appointments for out of school hours.

9 **Keep in touch.** If your child has to miss time off school through illness or bereavement, make sure you inform her teacher. The school will be concerned if they don't hear from you.

10 **Get help.** If truancy becomes a real problem, it might be time to ask for help. Work with the school to put things right. You can also rely on support from the education welfare officers at your local authority.

Work/life balance

Britain has the longest working hours in Europe. We might be enjoying higher earnings, but what is being sacrificed as a result? Overwork is forcing parents into unhealthy lifestyles as they attempt to reconcile long working hours and family responsibilities. Working long hours is also leading to a nation beset with stress, irritability, exhaustion and depression, none of which contribute to a loving home environment. Few of us have the finances to stop work altogether, so how can you steer your life towards a better balance?

1 **Do a family audit.** Look at the family budget. Work out where the family resources are being spent and write it all down. If you had to, could you manage on less income? Could you find a way to spend less on the car, on holidays or on house improvements if the prize were more time for your child and for yourself?

2 **Talk to your boss.** There may be a possibility of job sharing, working from home or going part-time. Employers have a legal obligation to take such requests seriously and can only reject them for good business reasons. It's important, however, that you make a convincing case for how much more productive you'll be if you can improve your current work situation.

3 **Consider a new career.** You might have to come to the difficult decision that your chosen career is simply not family friendly. Is it time to explore a new career that leaves more time for you and your loved ones?

4 **Make a sideways move.** If swapping careers is too drastic, is it possible to find a different job within your profession or company? Perhaps one with less responsibility or better working hours?

5 **Check your commuting time.** Is travelling time seriously eating into your family time? Would a house move or a job change reduce the journey time?

6 **Take your foot off the gas.** If life is constantly packed with scheduled activities, even at home, consider finding ways to slow down. Don't make plans for every evening or weekend – enjoy the sensation of making things up as you go along.

7 **Practise time management.** If you were more organized, would it free up more time for family activities? Do you waste time searching for things or procrastinating? Check out time-management tips at www.bbc.co.uk/health/healthy_living.

8 **Share the burden.** Working parents, especially mums, tend to take on too much responsibility. Get the whole family involved in chores, food preparation, holiday planning and other family responsibilities.

9 **Look into getting outside help.** If you were to bring in someone to help with cleaning or ironing, would it free up time to spend with your child? If you can afford to, do it.

10 **Forget perfection.** We're sold the idea of a 'perfect' home life. It's a myth. Give yourself a break and focus on the things you are doing right.

Zits

Also known as spots or acne, zits are the bane of most teenagers' lives. Not content with just being on the face, these pesky pimples pop up on the back, neck, chest and arms too. The skin's sebaceous glands secrete an excess of sebum, blocking hair follicles and causing spots. Most children grow out of them eventually, but in the meantime, there are lots of things your child can do to minimize the mayhem.

1 **Don't squeeze spots.** It's tempting to squeeze or pick spots, but tell your teen not to. It can cause inflammation, an infection or permanent scarring.

2 **Avoid aggressive washing.** Spots aren't caused by dirt, but it's wise to to avoid a build-up of bacteria. Encourage your child to keep his skin clean by using an unperfumed cleanser twice a day.

3 **Don't blame chocolate.** A healthy diet containing bags of fruit and vegetables is essential for clear, glowing skin, but the odd treat won't set off an attack.

4 **Avoid certain beauty products.** Defrizzing hair products, pomades, suntan oils, fake-tan lotions and certain shampoos can irritate the skin and cause acne. Your child should use natural products with a minimum of chemical ingredients.

5 **Reduce stress.** Tests and exams, plus problems at home and school, can all affect acne. Encourage your child to try tackling things one at a time and not let problems become overwhelming.

6 **Check medication.** Sometimes teenagers are prescribed contraceptive pills containing progestogen hormones, which can make acne worse. It may be possible for your family doctor to suggest another pill that reduces the risk of acne.

7 **Use over-the-counter products.** These help to clear up spots and mild acne, but usually contain a strong agent called benzoyl peroxide, so go for the mildest cream you can find. Natural tea-tree oil can be effective too, but try it on a small area first to test for any allergic reaction.

8 **Be patient.** It can take weeks to clear up a large area of mild acne with over-the-counter products. If there is no improvement after two months, get your teen to talk to a GP about specialist treatment.

9 **Use concealers.** Medical concealer sticks are useful, especially if they match your child's skin tone. Cosmetics conceal to some extent, but try to avoid oily foundation, or go for non-comedogenic (non-clogging) beauty products.

10 **Don't suffer alone.** Reassure your child that most teenagers go through a 'spotty stage' and come out the other side unscathed. For support and helpful advice check out the Acne Support Group's website (www. stopspots.org).

...toddlers
The Best Friends' Guide to Toddlers by Vicki Iovine (Bloomsbury, 1999)
A survival manual to the 'terrible twos' (and ones and threes), from the first step to the last blanket.

...starting school
Starting School by Allan & Janet Ahlberg (Puffin Books, 1990)
A charming story aimed at little ones about to start school. Perfect for calming anxieties and encouraging children to get excited about the big day.

...pre-teens
Talking to Tweenies by Elizabeth Hartley-Brewer (Hodder & Stoughton, 2005)
A pocket guide to getting it right before it gets rocky. *The* most valuable book for any parent with children aged 8–12.

...teenagers
Teen Angels: How to FInd Calm in the Storm of the Teenage Years by Dr Stephen Briers & Sacha Baveystock (BBC Books, 2006)
A no-nonsense guide that tells you how to create a supportive environment for your teens, overcome issues and maintain a strong relationship into adulthood.

...divorce
It's Not the End of the World by Judy Blume (Macmillan Children's Books, 1998)
A sensitive, well-written story about a child dealing with her parents' divorce. Ideal for older children and young teens.

...health
Baby and Child Healthcare: The Essential A–Z Home Reference to Children's Illnesses, Symptoms and Treatments by Dr Miriam Stoppard (Dorling Kindersley, 2001)
Set out in a handy A–Z format, there's bags of info on a wide range of ailments and how best to treat them.

...education

Help Your Child Succeed at School by Dr Dominic Wyse (Prentice Hall Life, 2007)
An incisive and informative guide to helping your child (from pre-schoolers to 18-year-olds) to get the best from school.

...diet

The Food Doctor for Babies and Children by Vicki Edgson (Collins & Brown, 2003)
Provides great info and yummy recipes on the foods and nutrients needed for optimum health at every stage of your child's development.

...sleep

Teach Your Child to Sleep: Solving Sleep Problems from Newborn through Childhood by Millpond Sleep Clinic (Hamlyn, 2005)
Highly recommended guide. Helps you to understand the nature of sleep problems and how to encourage your child to get a good night's rest.

...positive parenting

Happy Children through Positive Parenting by Elizabeth Hartley-Brewer (Vermilion, 2005)
An easy-to-read guide about helping children to grow up feeling secure and good about themselves, enabling them to gain positive self-esteem.

State Crime

WITHDRAWN

CRIME AND SOCIETY SERIES

Series editor: Hazel Croall

Published titles

Burglary, by R.I. Mawby

Armed Robbery, by Roger Matthews

Car Crime, by Claire Corbett

Sex Crime: Sex offending and society (2e) by Terry Thomas

Street Crime, by Simon Hallsworth

Hate Crime, by Nathan Hall

Murder: Social and historical approaches to understanding murder and murderers, by Shani D'Cruze, Sandra Walklate and Samantha Pegg

Fraud, by Alan Doig

Safety Crimes, by Steve Tombs and Dave Whyte

State Crime, by Alan Doig